LAWBREAKING LADIES

LAWBREAKING LADIES

50 TALES *of* DARING, DEFIANT, *and* DANGEROUS WOMEN *from* HISTORY

ERIKA OWEN

TILLER PRESS

NEW YORK   LONDON   TORONTO   SYDNEY   NEW DELHI

First Tiller Press hardcover edition February 2021

TILLER PRESS and colophon are trademarks of Simon & Schuster, Inc.

For information about special discounts for bulk purchases,
please contact Simon & Schuster Special Sales at 1-866-506-1949 or
business@simonandschuster.com.

The Simon & Schuster Speakers Bureau can bring authors to your live event.
For more information or to book an event, contact the Simon & Schuster Speakers
Bureau at 1-866-248-3049 or visit our website at www.simonspeakers.com.

Interior design by Patrick Sullivan and Jennifer Chung

Eye mask icon by Adrien Coquet/The Noun Project
Thief icon by André Renault/The Noun Project
Hand fan icon by Nikita Kozin/The Noun Project
Knife icon by Lilit Kalachyan/The Noun Project
Spades icon by imron boss/The Noun Project
Bottles, Woman in mask, Playing cards, Fan, Gun,
and Knife illustrations courtesy of The British Public Library

Illustrations by Alexander Wright

Manufactured in China

1 3 5 7 9 10 8 6 4 2

Library of Congress Cataloging-in-Publication Data has been applied for.

ISBN 978-1-9821-4708-2
ISBN 978-1-9821-4709-9 (ebook)

For Joseph:
You're my favorite thing

C O N T E N T S

INTRODUCTION

Accoording to the FBI, a violent crime occurred every 24.6 seconds in 2017.[1] Many of the women featured in this book committed this kind of crime, but there have been women throughout the ages whom one could consider criminal for entirely different reasons.

What constitutes a crime can vary. "Crimes" can refer to illegal acts that break a specific law and may be prosecuted. But there are also social crimes, if you will—the kind of norm-breaking or morally-frowned-upon activities that won't get you arrested, but *will* get you talked about or tarnish your reputation in the court of public opinion. This book delves into both kinds of crimes, and in the pages that follow, you will read fifty stories of little-known and legendary women—from gamblers and con women to pirates and serial killers—who made history for their lawbreaking ways from the fifteenth century all the way to the mid-1900s. Some of these women boldly revolted against restrictive gender roles, while others found notoriety from their heinous acts against others.

I chose to profile these women because they all have stories that are almost hard to believe. And not all of them were evil people—keep that in mind as you read. There are several lawbreaking ladies I find admirable, like the buffalo soldier Cathay Williams and "Stagecoach Mary" Fields, who was the first Black female star route mail carrier in the United States. They are two people with whom I'd love to have dinner and get to know better; both were important and fascinating members of their communities, despite violating the written and unwritten laws women were expected to abide by during their time.

In this book, I'll also introduce you to women who pose an interesting juxtaposition with regard to their professions. For instance, you'll read about a professional gambler who allegedly shot her ex-lover dead and then just pages later read about a woman who helped fund an entire performing arts center through her work running a casino in Las Vegas. Although these gambling gals led very different lives, both were enterprising women who forged unconventional careers for their respective times, and both were remarkable in their own right. Their stories also serve to show that while the title of this book may sound like you're in for hundreds of pages of grisly crime—which is *partly* true (there are certainly women featured in this book with whom I'd never want to cross paths)—I'll give you a break once in a while with a more uplifting tale.

BEING A WOMAN: THE FEMININE SILHOUETTE THROUGHOUT HISTORY

When it came to investigating crimes of yore, women were usually not the first suspects police considered. And when they were, juries often found it hard to imagine women committing murders, robberies, and other illegal acts. While women have historically not had it easy (far from it, in many situations), they did have a special kind of advantage in the courtroom.

"The fairer sex" is a phrase that dates as far back as 1676, when it appeared in the wonderfully titled book *The Art of Making Love: Or Rules for the Conduct of Ladies and Gallants in Their Amours* by Le Boulanger de Chalussay. Old-fashioned as it may be, this phrase also helps explain the treatment of many female criminals throughout history. Women involved in illegal activities often managed to escape authorities, arrests, and convictions based on their perceived charm and good looks (looking at you, Belle Starr). And, more often than not, the physical beauty of even the most hard-core lawbreakers was mentioned in news stories about them. All in all, women criminals were frequently treated differently than their male counterparts.

The outlaws of the Wild West are a great example. Although women like Lillian Smith, Pearl Hart, and Etta Place were investigated for their crimes, they always seemed to get off because they were the girlfriend or wife of a notorious male criminal—and were assumed to have innocent relations to their "more dangerous" partners.

The hardest thing to do while writing this book was to separate actual facts from marginally sexist accounts. Newspapers that reported the crimes of some of the women featured in this book often used their word counts to comment on the woman's relationships and appearance instead of just the facts. While this is frustrating for many reasons—women are far more than their looks or their partners, even when they've committed a crime—it is important to remember as you learn about the following murderers, madams, bootleggers, pirates, and others who appear in this book.

THE CHANGING TIDES
OF PUNISHABLE CRIMES

I think we can all agree that moral judgments of certain criminal activity have changed, um, a lot since we've entered the twenty-first century. For instance, the idea of legalizing sex work is now seen as empowering to many people. During the Prohibition era (1920–1933), making and selling alcohol was illegal and could result in jail time. Today, there may be some states and counties that have strict rules regarding when or if you can purchase alcohol, but drinking is a widely accepted social activity. That being said, I don't think there's any world in which being a sadistic serial killer will ever be justified.

Some chapters in this book explore seemingly fantastical roles we mainly see in works of fiction: pirates, outlaws, bandits, gangsters. But it's important to remember, as you read this, that the law looked a lot different then than it does now. This book is simply a transference of fact, and it is not my intention to make value judgments about the women featured here whose actions may not be considered illegal or immoral by today's standards. I'm simply here to highlight the fascinating and often overlooked stories of these complicated women, who also happened to be lawbreakers.

Okay, now that you've been prepped on what to expect in the following pages, buckle up. I hope you can regale your friends, family, and coworkers with these remarkable tales—from a fraud who stole millions of dollars by forging checks to a popular musical group comprised entirely of female prisoners—for years to come.

NOT JUST IN THE MOVIES

Watching pirate movies is a fun way to spend your Saturday night, but after seeing a few, one thing will become very clear: There aren't many female pirates who have been portrayed as badass leading women instead of secondary love-interest characters. Don't get me wrong: Throughout history, some women *did* find roles managing pirate ships after becoming the love interest of a captain or two. But do some digging, and you'll find that their love stories quickly become a sidebar to the positions they held on their pirate ships.

The women featured in this section come from all over the world: Sweden, China, Ireland, and Morocco, to name just a few countries. Some of these women fell into the world of piracy out of desperation, others fell into it because of love, and a few saw the pirate's life as an opportunity to increase their personal wealth. What they all have in common is that they were tough as nails—and they had to be, as you'll soon realize, to keep up with the rough-and-tumble crews of these ships.

Terms to Know

Pirate: Someone who actively hunts out other ships and raids them for valuables and money.

Privateer: Think of this as a "legal" pirate. People in this role raid ships, but are granted permission by the government to raid enemy ships encroaching on their territory during times of war.

Piracy: An act of robbery committed on a boat at sea.

Letter of marque: An official document that grants amnesty from piracy laws to a privateer.

Raid: The act of boarding another ship and taking valuables, while capturing, fighting, or killing those found on the ship.

Sloop: A small, square-rigged sailing warship with two or three masts.

Code of conduct: The rules of a ship that all pirates must follow while on board.

SAYYIDA AL-HURRA

The MUSLIM PIRATE QUEEN WHO CHALLENGED GENDER ROLES

—>••<—

Sayyida al-Hurra was so revered that no one knows her real name. The name by which she is referred to is actually more of a title: *al-Hurra* means "free woman" and was often given to a woman in power, which she was. As a pirate queen, she ruled Morocco for nearly thirty years.

Born in Granada, Spain, Sayyida al-Hurra and her family were forced out of the country by the Spanish monarchs Ferdinand and Isabella, who were on a mission to rid Spain of Muslims. Eventually, her family found refuge in Morocco, but this came with its own set of issues: The regions and kingdoms surrounding the country were being claimed by battles left and right. But Sayyida al-Hurra's father found a role as the ruler of Chefchaouen, an independent region in Morocco, and his prestigious position helped his daughter land the governor of Tétouan, Abu l'Hassan al-Mandari II, as a husband.

Sayyida al-Hurra's background in politics and intense interests in regional relations turned out to be a big help to her husband. The result was a partnership that was fairly uncommon for the time: a couple in power who ruled equally. Sayyida al-Hurra even played a larger role in directing the regional military than al-Mandari. Her strict directives earned her the nickname "The Iron Lady of the Arab-Muslim World." Upon al-Mandari's death in 1518, she gained the role of al-Hakimat Tétouan ("ruler of Tétouan") and joined the Barbarossan pirates of Tétouan.

She restructured the waterways to lead to her own personal

docks, giving her more control and surveillance of the western Mediterranean Sea. Geographically, Tétouan was in a location of privilege. With close proximity to Spain and Portugal, Sayyida al-Hurra was able to follow through on her promise to take down the same forces that exiled her family from Spain so many years ago. Raiding enemy ships and bringing the bounty to Tétouan helped catapult the city to become one of the most powerful in Morocco. In turn, the Spanish and Portuguese were forced to negotiate with Sayyida al-Hurra, not only to resume important trade and commercial opportunities for their countries but also to seek the safe return of her Spanish and Portuguese captives. During her reign, she was known for taking prisoners and using them as bargaining chips. She once even captured the Portuguese governor's wife.

She became the wife of the Moroccan sultan, Ahmed al-Wattassi, in 1541, but even in her remarriage, she remained in a seat of power. In another move that rebelled against tradition, she made al-Wattassi travel to *her* in Tétouan so they could get married, which was not something brides did at the time. Even after their marriage, Sayyida al-Hurra continued to live in Tétouan, where she ruled the city and maintained the agreements she had made with the Spanish and Portuguese. A year later, in 1542, she was removed from her reign by a rebel group, which reportedly included her stepson from her first marriage, Muhammad al-Hassan al-Mandri.

Sayyida al-Hurra was never arrested or imprisoned for her acts of piracy, and it arguably would have been a tough sell to do so given her high rank in Morocco and the power she brought to Tétouan. Despite her demise, though, her grit and determination deserve to be recognized.

JACQUOTTE "BACK FROM THE DEAD RED" DELAHAYE

The PIRATE WHO FAKED HER OWN DEATH

———◆➤••⟨◆———

When you look up Jacquotte Delahaye online, you're more likely to come across red wine blends and band names inspired by the look and acts of this French-Haitian pirate than her story, but it's a story worth learning. According to legend, Jacquotte's mother died in childbirth around 1600, and her father was murdered shortly after. Left without parents, Jacquotte became the caretaker of her younger brother, who was disabled. While there is not much information out there regarding what their life was like together, one can imagine how difficult it might have been. On the hunt for a stable income, Jacquotte turned to piracy, where she found community, respect, and wealth.

Jacquotte, with help from fellow strong-willed Frenchwoman Anne Dieu-le-Veut, eventually put together her own pirate crew. They commanded a handful of boats and set out plundering ships in the Caribbean. But soon, other pirate crews caught on to what they were doing and offered a reward to anyone who could take down Jacquotte.

Once she got word about the price that had been put on her head, Jacquotte faked her own death. Naturally, this meant stepping into retirement from her pirate lifestyle. But it didn't last long. She grew bored and decided to try piracy again, this time disguised as a man in an attempt to keep her identity safe from those who were looking to take her down. Her bright red hair was hard to hide, though, and eventually people caught on to her ruse. Once people knew she hadn't, in fact, died, they started calling her a new name: "Back from the Dead Red." Her general infamy and her perseverance against those who were searching for her left an impression. Instead of enemies, she gained followers.

Jacquotte led thousands of pirates around Haiti. She eventually found a small Caribbean island and turned it into an oasis for her plundering peers. Legend has it that she died protecting her paradise from other pirates.

INGELA GATHENHIELM

The SWEDISH PRIVATEER
WHO HAD the KING'S BLESSING

———◆≻••≺◆———

Ingela Gathenhielm was born in 1692 to Olof Hammar and Gunilla Mårtensdotter on a farm in Onsala, Sweden (a town located south of Gothenburg). In 1711, when she was nineteen years old, she was married in the local church to a man named Lars Gathe. One of the few things we know about Ingela and her family was that she was well-off—the brass chandelier her family donated to the Onsala church for her wedding can still be seen hanging in its gallery. Ingela and Lars had five children, but only two, Anders and Lars, lived long enough to reach adulthood. This may all seem like the relatively normal story of two people who started a family in Sweden in the midst of the Great Northern War. But that's only a small part of it.

Privateering was common across Europe during this time and

was defined as "using a privately owned armed vessel commissioned by a belligerent state to attack enemy ships, usually vessels of commerce."[1] Lars Gathe was a privateer who was given permission by King Charles XII of Sweden to target enemies traveling through the waters of the nearby Baltic Sea. He made quite a name (and fortune) for himself pillaging commerce ships and selling the stolen goods.

But back to Ingela: After her husband died in 1718, she took over his pirate empire and earned the nickname "The Shipping Queen," a title her father—also a shipowner in his time—surely would have been proud of.

Ingela's story is slightly different from the others you'll find in this book. While she wasn't arrested or jailed for her time as a pirate, she made a very successful career of it under the approving eye of the Swedish king. After Sweden signed a peace treaty with their forgiven enemy, Denmark, in 1720, ending the Great Northern War, Ingela hung up her pirate hat and married a Russian lieutenant by the name of Isak Browald. When she died in 1729, her body was returned to Onsala and buried next to the body of her son Lars.

ANNE BONNY

The PIRATE WHO PLEADED PREGNANT

M ost images depict Anne Bonny with a head of flaming red hair, a hard look in her eyes, and an especially sharp jawline. Her strong and intimidating beauty sets the scene for the massive cloud of mystery that surrounds this fiery Irish pirate who sailed the seas during the eighteenth century. A good deal of what we think we know about Anne comes from the book *A General History of the Pyrates* by Captain Charles Johnson. According to Johnson, Anne, born in Ireland's county Cork (her exact birth date has never been confirmed), was the result of an affair between William Cormac, a married Irish lawyer, and one of his housemaids. After Cormac's divorce, which ended up costing him most of his clientele, he brought Anne and her mother with him to what is now known as Charleston, South Carolina. Anne's mother contracted typhoid fever and passed away when Anne was thirteen, and Cormac attempted to pair Anne in marriage. She refused to comply, and in 1718 married a sailor by the name of John Bonny.

However, it wasn't with John that Anne entered into a life of piracy, so hold tight. As the story goes, Anne grew weary of John after sailing with him to the Bahamas, which was then a new territory. While John busied himself as an informant for the local Bahamian government, specifically for privateer Woodes Rogers, Anne found herself a new suitor—a pirate by the name of John Rackham, also known as "Calico Jack." (I'll refer to him by his nickname from here on out to avoid any confusion—it seems our friend Anne had a thing for Johns.) The new couple attempted to get Anne out of her marriage in an honest manner: Calico Jack offered to pay John to divorce Anne. But John wouldn't accept the offer. Without John's blessing, Anne joined Calico Jack in stealing and sailing the *William*, a single-masted ship, to New Providence, an island in the Bahamas. Along the way, Anne was introduced to the hobby that would make her famous: pirating.

There's something important to know about this time period in the pirate community: Having a woman aboard a ship was seen as unlucky. For this reason, it wasn't common for pirate ship commanders to partner up with women in the way Calico Jack and Anne did. And it wasn't uncommon for women who did join the crews of pirate ships to dress in disguise as men. While Anne did not hide her true identity from her fellow pirates, she dressed as a man when they pillaged ships, as well as when she partook in physical combat. Anne had a reputation for getting physical since long before she boarded the *William*. According to rumor, she had once beaten up an attempted rapist so badly, he needed to be hospitalized. Needless to say, Anne was perceived as a tough cookie, and her status as the ship commander's partner only added to her intimidating air.

Anne's notoriety was short-lived, though. In 1718, Woodes Rogers—who had by then acquired the title of governor of New Providence—reentered the picture. Pirating in New Providence was not new, or secret. Before Rogers created the local government, the area was a bit of a free-for-all. Laws were not written in stone, and people who were put on trial were at the mercy of how good or bad a judge's day was going. The happenings within the pirating community were often shared in local papers, and Anne's name was no stranger to their pages: A 1720 copy of the *Boston Gazette* refers to her as "Ann Fulford alias Bonny." When she teamed up with Calico Jack, an update in the same newspaper in October 1720 read that he "took with him 12 Men and Two Women."[1]

Rogers caught wind of the *William* and its increasing attacks on boats along the coast, and sent privateer Captain Jonathan Barnet to bring the ship's crew in. Barnet found the crew of the *William* all right, in a remote cove in Negril Point, Jamaica, but as the story goes, the pirates were all too drunk to fight back. In fact, the most delightful part of this story may be what a witness described the crew drinking: "a bowl of punch." Guns were fired, words were surely yelled, and it still wasn't enough. Anne Bonny and Mary Read, the only other woman working on the *William* at the time, were in on the action. But their efforts weren't enough to defeat Barnet. Nine members of the crew, including Anne and Mary, were captured and brought to Spanish Town, Jamaica, to stand trial.

The women's trial began on November 28, 1720. Anne was addressed as a " 'spinster' late 'of the Island of Providence.' "[2] During the trial, a number of witnesses who worked on the boats Anne had helped raid shared their stories of seeing her in action. Thomas Dillon, captain of a ship called the *Mary and Sarah*, had the most descriptive encounter with Anne: In the courtroom, he shared that after being reassured that the *William* was an English ship and safe to board, he was met on deck by Anne, who pulled a gun on him. He described both Anne and Mary Read as "both very profligate, cursing and swearing much, and very ready and willing to do anything on board."[3] After the courtroom heard a number of damning accounts of Anne's contributions aboard the *William*, she was sentenced to death by hanging along with her fellow pirates.

In the end, Anne (and Mary) got lucky. After being sentenced to death for their wrongdoings, the two women shared that they were both pregnant. This proclamation saved their lives, but both were jailed. Mary never made it out alive, dying in prison a handful of months later—some believe she died during childbirth, and it's unclear if the child survived. Anne, however, was released, though no one can confirm whether or not she was actually pregnant. Many think it was the influence of her father (he was a lawyer, remember) that garnered her her freedom.

Anne's story gets a bit blurry post-prison. As exciting as her life at sea had been, many believe that Anne once again put down roots in Charleston, married, and had children. No matter what actually happened, it sure is fun to imagine that someone out there may have a great-great-great-great-grandmother with a thrilling swashbuckling past.

RACHEL WALL

The PIRATE HANGED *for a* CRIME SHE DIDN'T COMMIT

'm going to skip ahead a couple of years into Rachel Wall's life and kick off this story with a picture of the Pennsylvania-born woman at the age of sixteen. It was at this time Rachel left her family and made moves to the east to be closer to the coast, which I'll call the catalyst for her pirating ways. It was on one particular adventure that she met George Wall, a fisherman, and journeyed to Philadelphia, New York, and Boston with him. At a certain point in Boston, for reasons that are not completely confirmed by historians, Rachel and George parted ways. Rachel stayed to take on work as a domestic servant in the well-off neighborhood of Beacon Hill, while George left the city—but it certainly wasn't the last she would see of him.

George returned to Boston in 1782 and convinced Rachel to join him in a career change of sorts: piracy. The couple embarked on a life of raiding ships, first attacking a boat named the *Essex* and claiming it as their own. To catch the attention of passing ships, they would disguise the *Essex* to look as if it were damaged. Rachel would call out to nearby ships for help, luring them to tie up to the *Essex* and aid its two-person crew. Once the boat was securely attached, Rachel and George would board the unsuspecting ship, deal with the crew, and take all the valuables they had to offer. Together, they raided at least twelve ships—and took the lives of no less than twenty-four sailors.

However, they hit a bout of bad luck later that year, when the

Essex encountered a storm. George, along with other members of the crew, drowned when the ship wrecked. Rachel survived.

Rachel returned to Boston and continued to raid ships, though in a less conspicuous manner. She would board the boats while their crews slept, stealing from right under their noses. Throughout her pirating career, Rachel was charged with numerous counts of petty theft, as well as larceny. As ironic as it may be, her final and lethal charge was for something she didn't actually do. In March 1789, Margaret Bender, a seventeen-year-old Rachel had encountered while walking along a road, accused Rachel of stealing her bonnet, shoes, and buckles. Because the alleged crime took place on a road, it was considered highway robbery. Throughout the trial, Rachel denied ever having robbed Margaret, though she did confess to several acts of piracy. She was found guilty and hanged on October 8, 1789, in front of a massive crowd.

CHING SHIH

The FORMIDABLE PIRATE PRINCESS

I f you've gone your entire lifetime and never heard the name Ching Shih, then . . . okay, I won't hold it against you. But you may regret not knowing her epic story sooner. Born in 1775 as Shi Xianggu, Ching Shih came to be known as one of the world's most iconic pirates in her sixty-nine years on Earth. While little is known about her early life—we do know that her name, Ching Shih, translates to "Widow of Cheng"—her historic journey begins in the

Guangdong Province of China on a floating brothel. It was here, working as a sex worker, that Ching Shih met her future husband, the well-known pirate Cheng Yi.

To set the scene, floating brothels like the one on which Ching Shih worked were massive wooden structures—often referred to as "flower boats"—that housed a handful of women who were paid to perform sexual acts. Some of the boats only serviced Chinese people, while others welcomed foreigners. The local government had strict rules regarding the existence of these floating brothels. According to Paul A. Van Dyke's research in "Floating Brothels and the Canton Flower Boats 1750–1930," being a boat owner came with its share of hefty expenses. "The freedom to provide sexual services in the Pearl River Delta did not come without a price," he wrote.[1] The boats at Whampoa Island and their counterparts in other locations had to pay regular fees to local authorities. There are a number of stories that recount how Cheng Yi and Ching Shih met, but it's likely they had an encounter on one of these boats during a pirate raid led by Cheng's troupe.

Ching Shih's adventurous life began after she married Cheng Yi. Once she became his wife, she was entitled to 50 percent of his bounty and also became the mother of his adopted son, Cheung Po Tsai. She proved herself a worthy partner, too, quickly becoming more well-known than her husband. And that is saying something. Cheng Yi had been given an honorary title, "Golden Dragon of the Imperial Staff," by the emperor. This role made Cheng Yi a prince, and thus made Ching Shih a princess.

When Cheng Yi died suddenly six years into their marriage, Ching Shih took control of his fleet of 1,800 pirate ships, which was referred to as the Red Flag Fleet. Her quiet and deliberate nature as the leader of this fleet was very different from what Cheng Yi's captains were used to dealing with, as he had been boisterous and impulsive, but many believe that Ching Shih's purposeful ways served her well, especially in her choice of a second husband: Cheung Po Tsai . . . her stepson, who had been her late husband's go-to captain.

There were two bright sides to this partnership for Ching Shih: Cheung Po Tsai was highly regarded and respected by the fleet's captains. He also wasn't the most educated sailor, unlike Ching Shih, so she was able to easily influence him while ruling over the fleet.

Over time, she developed a decidedly severe code of conduct as a leader, which may have been what gained her the most notoriety. Sailors within her fleet had to get her approval before any and all raids—if they failed to do so, they would be beheaded. Everything that was stolen had to be reported to the sailor's superior, and if it wasn't, the offender would be beaten. Sailors who broke this rule twice would lose their life. If someone fled or left their post to go ashore without permission, his ears would be cut off; a second offense would earn him a death sentence. The word "plunder" was also not allowed on board; the fleet was directed to use the phrase "transferring shipment of goods" in its place.

Among these strict rules, however, were a few that stood out as fairly progressive for the time and place. If Ching Shih discovered that any of her sailors had raped a female captive, the sailor would lose his head. Even what sailors considered to be "consensual" sex with a female captive had to be approved by Ching Shih. If a sailor wanted to earn Ching Shih's approval on this front, he would have to take the prisoner as his wife, treat her well, and remain faithful to her. If he failed to obtain Ching Shih's permission and the act still occurred, the sailor would be beheaded and the female captive would be thrown overboard while tied to a lead weight.

As a pirate, Ching Shih became such a nuisance to the Chinese government that in 1809 it sent out a series of boats (deemed "suicide ships") that were full of straw and explosives in an attempt to kill her. But she outsmarted them and their assassination attempt.

The Red Flag Fleet ended up extinguishing the burning suicide ships, repairing them, and taking them for their own.

Despite wanting her dead at one point, the Chinese government ultimately helped Ching Shih retire from the pirate's life, dismissing their warrants for her arrest and sending her off with a big wad of cash after she negotiated her own capture in return for the safety of her captains and shipmates. Ching Shih died at the age of sixty-nine, having run a brothel and gambling room in the final years of her remarkable life.

SADIE "THE GOAT" FARRELL

The HEAD-BUTTING PIRATE

⬦••⬥

P irates don't just sail the seven seas—there are also communities of "river pirates" who work the smaller waterways that wind through various countries. Sadie Farrell, known to many as "The Goat," was part of one such group in the United States.

Born and raised in New York City in the Fourth Ward, near the East River, by 1869 Sadie had made a name for herself with the local thieves and street hustlers. Her own thieving began by targeting drunks stumbling out of the local bars near the docks. Her method was . . . strange, to say the least, and ultimately earned Sadie her nickname. Once she had her eye on a poor soul, she would run at them and ram her head into their stomach to catch them off guard. Sadie always worked with a male companion, who would nail the victim in the head with a rock via slingshot once Sadie had done her initial damage. Once the drunkard was unconscious, the duo would steal everything he had on him. It was this move, done again and again and again, that put Sadie's name on the lips of criminals around town.

In one of her most storied encounters, Sadie squared up with a bouncer at the Hole-in-the-Wall bar after having a few too many drinks herself. The bouncer's name was Gallus Mag—a nickname, as her real name is unknown—a six-foot-tall Irishwoman known for the cruel and unusual treatment she doled out to unruly patrons. If you didn't calm down after one or two of her warnings (which were often accompanied by a hit from a belt or a knock on the head), Mag would grab you by the head, bite off part of your ear, and toss you out the door. Your ear would then go in a jar labeled "Gallus Mag's Trophy Case." Sadie's encounter with Mag was a meeting of the minds, so to speak, given Sadie's own unusual method of fighting. But it was Mag who won this battle. She swiftly ripped off Sadie's ear, dropped it in an alcohol-filled jar, and labeled it "Sadie the Goat's Ear."

After this humiliating upset, Sadie took her talents across town to the docks on Manhattan's West Side. There she watched the Charlton Street Gang unsuccessfully attempt to raid a ship docked in what is now the Hudson. She talked the failed pirates into letting her lead their next attack, and just days later, they targeted a large sloop. It was an invasion that kicked off a life of pirating for Sadie and her gang.

Once they overcame the ship and its crew, Sadie and the Charlton Street Gang raised a skull-and-crossbones flag (known as the Jolly Roger) up the mast and took off into the North and Harlem Rivers. These waterways carried the crew to Poughkeepsie and beyond. They took their pirating to land, taking over small towns and villages, raiding homes for valuables, and ransacking mansions along the coast. The one thing Sadie and the rest of the gang avoided were major ocean liners—they were far too well protected for the small group and their amateur pirating to penetrate.

By the late 1800s, pirates had been scouring the water for a long time. There were already tales of long-dead pirates and their larger-than-life raids. Sadie really became the role and dug into the history of and embodied the monstrous pirates who had parted the seas before her. She was known to send her crew to "walk the plank" if they disobeyed her, a punishment associated with pirate crews from long ago. When she discovered that Julius Caesar had once been kidnapped by pirates, she tasked her crew with a kidnapping spree of their own.

The murders and raids ended when a group of residents from New York's Hudson Valley teamed up with the local police to ambush the Charlton Street Gang as they were targeting small merchant ships sailing on the North River. A good chunk of Sadie's crew was killed in this attack, sending her and the remaining crew members back to the West Side docks in New York City. After they officially disbanded, Sadie returned to the Fourth Ward with a new nickname: "Queen of the Waterfront." With her reputation—and the money she had raised during her career as a pirate—she opened a gin mill.

This story has a quirky, full-circle ending. You remember the Hole-in-the-Wall bar, where Sadie had part of her ear bitten off by Gallus Mag? Well, that bar was home to seven murders in just two months. Understandably, the New York City police shut it down. But before the doors officially closed, Sadie went to visit Gallus Mag. Legend has it, the two women settled their score. To mark the occasion, Gallus hopped over the bar, grabbed the jar that held Sadie's ear, and gave it back to her—very much pickled at this point.

I don't know if I quite believe this next part, but it's worth sharing, if only for the visual: The story goes that Sadie wore her severed ear in a locket around her neck up until the day she died.

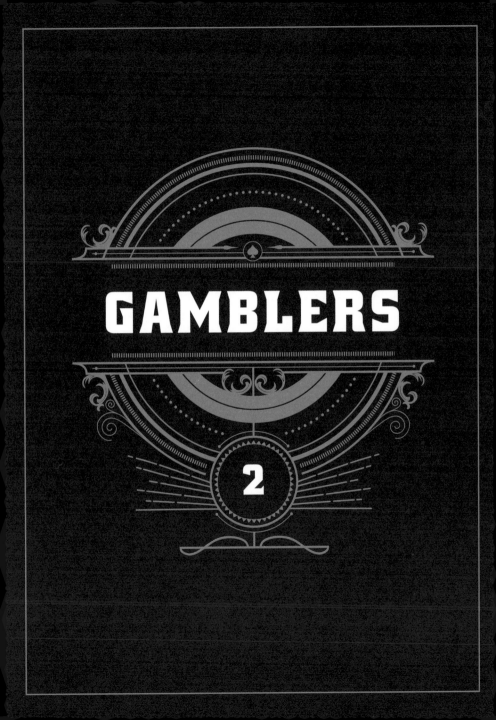

WOMEN WITH A RICH HISTORY

L et's look way back into history—I'm talking 4,500 to 5,000 years ago—and consider where gambling began. Those living in Egypt, China, Greece, and India, for instance, spent hours playing cards and games of chance long before the first controlled gambling facility was introduced in Rome in 1638. Chinese gamblers have been playing games of chance with tiles and dice since 2500 BCE. But as you can imagine, gambling has not been the same experience for men and women.

Take Rome as an example: Women were only allowed to gamble on certain occasions, such as during Bona Dea—a secret festival for married women honoring the Italian deity of the same name that consisted of eating, dancing, gaming, and music—while men could partake whenever they wanted.

With the introduction of the French game faro, a card game of chance made up of a banker and several players, to the Wild West, women began making more of an impact in the gambling world. Many of these women were involved in other illegal activities that put them on the radar of local authorities, too. Brothels doubled as gaming dens in some cases, the madams serving as card dealers. At different times throughout history, both gambling and owning a brothel were legal, but they more often than not came with their fair share of arrests due to the myriad bad behaviors they inspired.

While gambling has had a presence throughout most of history, an especially intriguing community of women who gambled existed in the eighteenth century. At the time, gambling halls usually followed commercial success, and notably mining—meaning, wherever you found people striking gold, you would also find people winning and losing it at a card table. While women were not often convening in these gaming halls, there were quite a few female characters who made their mark on the scene, either as card dealers, cardplayers, entertainment, or all of the above.

The women whose stories are told in this section were active in the eighteenth century and onward. They were charming, steadfast, and whip-smart in a time when women were more often expected to keep their opinions close and quiet.

Terms to Know

Faro: A card game played by guessing the order in which cards will appear; very popular during the Wild West era.

Gaming room/gambling hall: A recreational hall that hosts card games; usually run by men, it was also common to dance, drink, and meet women at these halls.

Deadwood: A city in South Dakota that was a popular place for cowboys, gambling halls, and gold mining.

Numbers racket: An early form of the lottery, originating in Italy, that required players to pick numbers that matched an assortment of randomly chosen numbers.

MARIA GERTRUDIS "LA TULES" BARCELÓ

SANTA FE'S SAVING GRACE

When the Santa Fe Trail was established in 1821, Maria Gertrudis Barceló saw an opportunity. Her knack for dealing cards gained her a sort of regional fame among travelers along the route between Franklin, Missouri, and Santa Fe, New Mexico. Maria was born into a prosperous family of Spanish ranchers and received a great education for a woman in the mid-1800s. She married Don Manuel Antonio Sisneros at the age of twenty-three—but broke tradition and kept her home, her dowry, and her maiden name, which was a completely uncommon move for the time. Together, they had two children, but sadly lost both kids in their infancy.

In 1825, the couple opened up a small gambling operation near a mining camp in Santa Fe. Maria's game of choice was called monte. To play, the dealer would ask the player to bet a sum of money to see if they could find the money card in a group of three cards. It was quick, easy to play, and hard to win—the perfect equation for miners looking to let off some steam after a long day of work. Maria moved on to launch her own gambling hall in the Ortiz Mountains, but soon after opening the new establishment, the Mexican authorities fined Maria for running an illegal gambling den. However, that didn't stop her from continuing to develop her own card-dealing skills.

The gambling setup in the mountains ultimately helped Maria, who had by then picked up the nickname "La Tules" for her willowy figure (*tules* is Spanish for "reed"), amass the funds to move into Santa Fe, which was a much more serious—and safer, given that registered casinos were legal to operate there—location for a gambling hall business. She bought a hotel and casino after she arrived, signing the deed with her own name and no mention of her husband.

The building was massive, spanning an entire block between Palace Avenue and San Francisco Street on Burro Alley. On the inside, Maria went all out decorating the space in the finest carpets, linens, lighting, and furnishings. Maria hired men to sing and couples to dance a traditional two-person jig called the fandango among the gamblers. The hotel-casino was known as a recreational hub for anyone and everyone—there was no social class, wealth, or race required to get in the front door. While she was running her hotel and casino, Maria dabbled in real estate and gold, and bets at her table in the casino were also a gold mine, as many would pay the high stakes just to be in her presence.

All in all, Maria became a very rich person—but she didn't keep her earnings all to herself. She was a frequent donor to the Catholic Church, as well as to local families in need. She and her husband adopted two girls into their family, though there is no record of what year this happened. Maria's place in society had climbed so much that Manuel Armijo—New Mexico's governor at the time—was even the godfather of one of her daughters.

When the Mexican–American War reached New Mexico in 1846, Maria played a key role in welcoming American troops to the state. Recognizing that the Americans would have a growing authority over the land and knowing she would soon need to adapt, Maria started to work as a spy for the Americans. As a card dealer, she interacted with a lot of people and thus gathered a lot of information. She would pass some of that information to the Americans, as well as alert them to various conspiracies among the Mexican troops. She also contributed money to the American war effort by buying the soldiers food.

Extravagant dinners were held at her home, gaining her even more points from the Americans.

As a result of her allegiance to the Americans, though, some people deemed Maria a traitor to Mexico's cause and began spreading unseemly rumors, like that she was a "prostitute" or had engaged in an affair with Governor Armijo. Many of the rumors about Maria also swirled among the Americans who were passing through Santa Fe, and she was bad-mouthed in American newspapers—something she would not have known, given that she only spoke Spanish. She was known for taking people to court if they spoke ill of her, and one can imagine that she would have done so had she been aware of the gossip swirling in American papers.

When the war ended in 1848, Maria continued to run her hotel and casino, and in 1849 she became a United States citizen. She continued living in Santa Fe until her death on January 17, 1852. As in life, she donated a hefty amount of money to charities upon her death, and left her property and additional funds to her remaining family members. While a fine for running an illegal gambling den may have made her a lawbreaking lady, she had a huge, charitable heart.

ELEANOR "MADAME MOUSTACHE" DUMONT

The GAMBLER WHO FELL VICTIM to a BROKEN HEART

———◆>••<◆———

Not much is known about Eleanor Dumont's early life. She was born Simone Jules, but changed her name to the arguably more elegant-sounding Eleanor Dumont after searching for a new start later in life.

Her father was a viscount who lost control of his finances after Napoleon fell, and some accounts purport that she may have been forced into an arranged marriage in an attempt to regain her family's status. However, this marriage was said to have gone bad after she had an affair with a lieutenant, for which she was imprisoned inside her home. To get to California, Eleanor would have had to escape from her home—many accounts believe she was born in New Orleans—but the details on how she made the trip are even foggier.

She could often be found at Bella Union's *vingt-et-un* ("twenty-one," which was a predecessor to blackjack) table where she also dealt cards. Players knew her for her calm demeanor under stress, as well as her elegant and aloof personality. It was here that she made the beginnings of a name for herself, winning a significant amount of money. But because of this, she was let go from her job after being accused of "sharping cards," or winning through deception.

It was at that point, after moving on to Nevada City, that Eleanor made the name change I mentioned earlier. And the name matched her elegant appearance. Nevada City was full of gold miners with

money to spend—a great entrepreneurial opportunity for Eleanor, given her skills. She would walk the streets to take in the empty business fronts, all while envisioning a gambling den of her very own. It also made quite the fodder for town gossip, as many wondered what the finely dressed out-of-towner was doing peering into their storefronts. It wasn't until she put an ad in the paper promoting the "best gambling emporium in northern California"[1] that people began to get an idea of what was to come. Shortly after, locals began receiving an invite to the grand opening of the Vingt-et-un, which was named after the card game Eleanor loved and at which she excelled. The invite promised free champagne for the first game, an effective enticement even by today's standards.

The new gambling den, complete with fine furnishings and gaspowered chandeliers, was marketed toward well-groomed men. Even more, Eleanor kept rare liquors and wines stocked at the bar, which drew in customers from across the region. All this may seem like a perfectly acceptable way to start a business . . . in the twenty-first century. But by societal standards in the mid-1800s, this was *not* a career a woman should have pursued. The announcement of Eleanor's new endeavor raised more than a few eyebrows. But undeterred, she moved forward.

Eleanor herself could be found dealing cards at the twenty-one table most nights. Her charm would soften the blow of a player's loss, as she often struck up lively conversation with her customers to keep them playing. She was known for one nicety in particular: When someone ran out of money at her table, she would buy them a glass of milk or treat them to champagne. (If that's not a power move, I don't know what is.)

In 1854, as the club's popularity grew, Eleanor brought on a partner to help her manage Vingt-et-un. He was a professional gambler from New York City by the name of David Tobin. Together, they also opened another den called Dumont's Palace, which specialized in faro and chuck-a-luck, a game of chance (as the name suggests) played with three dice. Dumont's Palace became an entertainment hub as well, and the pair hired musicians to keep the gamblers entertained between games. Needless to say, it was a hit.

Professionally, Eleanor skyrocketed the two years she was in Nevada City. Personally . . . things could have been better. While she could have had her choice of suitors from among the many men who tried to woo her at the card tables, she set her eyes on an editor of the local *Nevada Journal*: Edwin G. Waite—who happened to be the same editor to whom she submitted the ad announcing the grand opening of the Vingt-et-un. They had a special connection, as he reportedly often called on her and visited her room late at night, but a full-bodied romance never resulted, due to her unreciprocated feelings for him.

Despite this, her unrequited love for Edwin never worked against her in a truly damaging way until he married a woman he determined to be "socially acceptable." This was the ultimate gut punch for Eleanor. In her despair, she began drinking heavily. She also turned her professional relationship with her business partner, David Tobin, into a personal one, and it wasn't long before she uncovered his dark intentions. He not only tried to take over Eleanor's business, but he also beat her behind closed doors.

Remember: Eleanor was an unlikely business owner, given the time and place. And she didn't stay down for long. In 1857, she fired her partner, sold her business, and made her way to Columbia, California, where she began life anew.

In her new home, Eleanor set up a gambling table inside a hotel. She kept this up for a few years, dealing cards and making a good living from her skills. But after a while, she made the decision to step away from gambling and try a new lifestyle. She bought a ranch in Carson City, Nevada, but knowing no one in the area, she became lonely fairly quickly, which led to the third doomed relationship in her life: Jack McKnight, a cattle buyer. He was well-dressed and hand-some, and it didn't take Eleanor long to fall for his charms. But their relationship only lasted about a month before Jack disappeared with her money—including what he got for selling her ranch from under her feet. But karma intervened: Eleanor hunted him down and shot him dead a few days later, according to legend. All potential or fac-tual story lines aside, his robbery forced Eleanor to get back into gambling as a means of piecing her life back together, financially. And this is where Eleanor's journey leads her to the Comstock Lode, a mass of silver that was discovered along the eastern edge of Mount Davidson.

In the late 1850s, boom towns had begun popping up throughout mountainous regions in California, in accordance with wherever the latest lode of silver had been found. Eleanor, being the entrepreneur she was, kept a close eye on the discoveries and became a well-known character in the mining camps along the hot strike areas. It was at this point she swapped out her drink of choice—wine—for something a bit harder: whiskey and brandy. Where she was once the subject of many romance fantasies, she became what we could equate to "one of the guys." She also became known for the hair that had begun to grow on her upper lip, which led to her being dubbed "Madame Moustache." It only took one poor sport's utterance of the nickname after suffering a particularly rough loss for it to stick.

In her later years, Eleanor shifted from gambling to sex work, eventually owning a brothel at some point in the 1860s. She was known for employing the most beautiful women in the cities of Fort Benton and Bannack, Montana. Aside from the part where she may or may not have shot one of her ex-lovers dead, this is another area in which she smashed societal expectations. As you'll learn a bit later on in this book, owning a brothel was not the easiest or most socially accepted business endeavor—it often came with big fines and, oc-casionally, even jail time.

In the 1870s, Eleanor spent some time in Deadwood, South Dakota. While her activity in the area didn't skew from what she was usually up to (gambling!), some say that she struck up a friendship with another important lady of the time: Calamity Jane. At fifty years old, Eleanor made her second-biggest move, to Bodie, California. This was also the last move of her life. She didn't stop dealing cards and she didn't stop playing, but a deep depression made her contemplate the greater losses in her life. She began to lose money, and with no business to bring in more—and a penchant for paying off every loss that came her way—Eleanor's situation worsened. Her last game of cards was played with $300 borrowed from a friend . . . and she lost. It was after this game that she took a walk into the desert of Northern California, where she drank red wine mixed with a fatal dose of morphine.

Her body was found the morning of September 8, 1879, with a note sharing that she was "tired of life" and requesting to be buried next to her first love: Edwin. While the community did come together to have Eleanor buried, they didn't send her back to Nevada City. Her grave can still be visited in Bodie.

BELLE SIDDONS

The SPY WHO GAMBLED

elle Siddons may have been the name she was born with, but those who played with her (or were played by her) would have known her as Luraine Monteverde or Madame Vestal. She also might just win the award for Most Versatile Woman Profiled in This Book. While she was surely famous for her card playing, she was also a stage performer of satirical songs and an underground surgeon who was just as likely to remove a bullet as she was to treat a drug overdose. But let's paint a picture of the woman who could seemingly do it all before we get into her lawbreaking.

Belle had long black hair that was often pinned back with luxurious hair clips. She was raised within a powerful political family in Jefferson City, Missouri, which gave her every advantage a woman could possibly have in the mid-1800s (a good education, familial support, wealth). She donned rich, velvet outfits and scads of costume jewelry, creating a scene that people couldn't help but notice. She was also charming, a personality trait hammered into her psyche as a young woman growing up in the antebellum South. It was the mix of her charm, arrestingly good looks, and soft-spoken elegance that gave way to an air of mystery noted by everyone who shared a gaming room with her.

It's odd that her first arrest wasn't for anything associated with gambling, but rather under the accusation of being a spy. Before opening her den, she used her charm to woo young men fighting in the Civil War, and often played the role of escort to, first, her Southern brethren and, second, the enemy Northern soldiers. General Samuel Ryan Curtis first ordered her arrest and later was accountable for holding her in jail for a few months (there's no widely accepted consensus for exactly how long she was there). She was eventually released in a prisoner exchange and made to promise that she would stick to hospital work, but the promise was short-lived.

After being freed by her Northern captors, she returned to Missouri and found a partner in Newt Hallett, a handsome surgeon from Kansas City. The couple moved to Texas, but the romance didn't last: A few years after moving south, her husband died of yellow fever. It was here that any conversation around her life as a wife, a prisoner of the North, or the daughter of a politically influential family in Jefferson City ended. From here on out, Belle Siddons became Madame Vestal. She traveled across the country playing faro, the card game that was made popular in France during the late seventeenth century and had become a favorite of gamblers across the Wild West.

Belle landed in Deadwood, South Dakota, arguably the central hub of gambling in the United States at the time. She opened up her own gaming room, and as you can imagine, a woman with her own gaming business caused talk among locals and those who traveled to see her setup. Belle neither confirmed nor denied the rumors that she was a young widow, which only added to her mysterious reputation.

Eventually, she caught the eye of Archie Cummings, a "guerilla raider of the Kansas frontier" with ties to a handful of roving gangs. Belle, who just couldn't stay away from a rebellious lifestyle, added "spy" to her résumé once more, sharing any information that came through her gaming room with Archie and, in turn, the gangs he ran with. For this information, she received a share of whatever the gangs would loot, as arranged by Archie. Throughout their partnership, Belle and Archie always held out for the dream of leaving Deadwood and starting a life elsewhere. But once they began to act on it, the plan started to fall apart.

This is where Boone May comes into the story. Boone, a lawman, was hired to clean out the gangs working along the Deadwood train line—and he certainly had Belle on his radar. By disguising himself as a rogue gunman, he wiggled his way into Belle's line of sight, eventually learning of her departure plans with Archie. She told him when Archie was heading to the train with her safe and a ticket to San Francisco, where she was to eventually meet him.

Archie and two of his men were stopped in their tracks by local police as soon as they got to the train station in Deadwood—Boone had sent a telegram to the station, alerting the authorities of their arrival. Archie and one of his men, Billy Mansfield, were captured and sent to Deadwood to await trial. But along the way, they were kidnapped by vigilantes, who hung them both from a cottonwood tree.

The story gets even more tragic from here. Belle attempted to take her own life by ingesting poison, but survived thanks to a doctor who reversed the poison's effects in time. However, the grief changed her. Gone were the elegant mannerisms and luxe outfits. In their place, there was a hardness to her personality and the ability to drink any other gambler under the table. The motivation to find and murder everyone involved in Archie's death seemed to drive Belle. She lived out her days drinking, smoking opium, gambling, and finding a fight wherever she went—a stark contrast to the refined woman she once was. She may not have the loud bang of a reputation of some of her Wild West neighbors, but Belle gave a new face to the rebellious woman living on her own terms during this time in history.

LOTTIE DENO

The FARO QUEEN WHO CHARMED the SOUTH

—————◆>••<◆—————

The daughter of a part-time gambler, Lottie Deno was destined to become a legend of the Wild West five-card-draw scene. She was born Carlotta J. Thompkins in Warsaw, Kentucky, on April 21, 1844. Her parents were wealthy, having earned themselves a substantial amount of money from tobacco farming, and Lottie and her younger sister were given the best education offered to women at the time, at an Episcopalian convent, as well as ample opportunities to travel due to her father's many business trips. Aside from his career as a tobacco farmer and horse breeder, Lottie's father was also a gambler and taught her everything she knew about card games. Lottie's father often traveled to New Orleans, bringing his daughters along for the ride. Given that there was a curfew for women at the time, though, he was only able to explore the city's many gambling facilities alone after dark. Lottie visited New Orleans multiple times up until 1861, when her father died in battle, fighting for the Confederate Army. Lottie was only seventeen years old.

At the time of her father's death, Lottie's mother's health also became an issue. Lottie was given the task of running the family's tobacco plantation, an unheard-of assignment for a woman her age at the time—and some of her extended family members were not pleased. A handful of Lottie's relatives decided that she would be better off living with family in Detroit, in a more appropriate setting. Her mother, with hopes that Lottie would meet someone to marry, allowed it. So off Lottie went, along with her nanny—a seven-foot-tall woman by the name of Mary Poindexter—as a chaperone, to start a new life states away.

In Detroit, Lottie's lifestyle was different. Instead of gambling, she made friends and attended parties. But the money her mother had sent her away with was quickly depleted and could not be renewed, as the war had taken its toll on the tobacco plantation and her mother and sister were struggling to stay afloat. It was time for Lottie to find a job. Luckily for her, she was invited to visit a gambling fraternity.

You can imagine what happened next: Lottie played, she won, and then she sent money home. It went on like this for a while, and no one asked any questions. And the family was better for it—Lottie came from a pious home, and winning hands of poker would not have been received well. Her mother's dream for her was simply to meet a wealthy, upstanding, Christian man to marry, but that hope was shattered when Lottie made the acquaintance of Johnny Golden, a Jewish gambler from Boston. Johnny and Lottie formed an unlikely pair, given that this was a time when mixed-faith relationships were widely frowned upon. But this wasn't what led to their breakup. The real kicker: Johnny just wasn't as good at card playing as Lottie was. They parted ways and both left Detroit, Johnny to the east and Lottie to New Orleans.

Shortly after arriving, Lottie learned of her mother's death back home in Kentucky, and in an effort to provide for her sister, Lottie took on steady work playing cards on riverboats throughout the southeastern United States. She made enough money to put her sister through private school.

Once her sister graduated in May 1865, Lottie paid for her to meet Lottie in San Antonio, Texas, the next stop on her journey. One of the things that drew Lottie to San Antonio was the lack of curfew for women: A person could gamble at any hour of the day, regardless of their gender.

Lottie played her way into a job after frequenting the Cosmopolitan Club—an upscale saloon near Alamo Plaza—but the gig was not at the club itself. The owner of another spot in town, the University Club, spotted her skills and asked her to come on as a house gambler. This meant she was hired to gamble at the club—and lure fellow players to come join her game. If she won, the club made money, and she took home a cut of the winnings. After accepting the job, Lottie had no shortage of opponents. Seeing a woman inside a gambling club was still a shock in the late 1860s, and she was reported to be a beautiful woman with large eyes who dressed in the most fashionable clothes. Her beauty and intrigue acted as a spell of sorts; people wanted to be around her. You would most commonly spot her at the five-card-draw table, but she was also quite skilled at the French game faro. Her beauty, combined with her affinity for card games, earned Lottie the nickname "Angel of San Antonio." All the while, Mary Poindexter would sit perched on a stool behind her, taking in the sorry scene of Lottie taking down opponent after opponent.

The man who hired Lottie at the University Club was Frank Thurmond. The two struck up a romance that only fizzled when Frank had to get out of town after stabbing and killing a patron at the club who had become disorderly. Lottie set out on a mission to find him, and when rumors pointed her west, she landed in Fort Concho, Texas, in search of more funds. Again, she stepped into a new saloon where she quickly made a name for herself. She also picked up a new nickname: Mystic Maude, which referred to her elusiveness after being asked what she was doing in the area. As you can imagine, claiming to be on the hunt for someone who had committed a crime would bring unwanted attention—for her and for Frank.

After she played out Fort Concho, she moved on to other towns in Texas: Jacksboro, Fort Worth, San Angelo, and Dennison. Given her habit of hopping from town to town, many (correctly) believed she was searching for a man to meet her at some point. Others assumed she was an outlaw. One thing many believed was that she was a cheat, conning people out of money across the United States. It was during a night of immense winning in Fort Griffin, Texas, that Lottie came into the nickname we associate with her today. As the legend goes, she once beat every single opponent she could at poker, and at the end of it all, a drunken patron shouted for her to change her name to "Lotta Dinero." She took his suggestion—well, a variation of it—and Lottie Deno was born. This moniker helped separate her career from her religious family as well.

Compared to the other cities Lottie played in, Fort Griffin was seedier, full of angry ex-soldiers and few women with good intentions. But there was one person in Fort Griffin Lottie didn't expect to see: Frank Thurmond. Disguised as a bartender at the Bee Hive Saloon and going by the name Mike Fogarty, Frank had managed to find a corner of the south where he could work and live undetected as the killer of that unruly patron at the University Club. Lottie also hosted a regular card game at the bar, under the watchful and admiring eye of Frank. The two would meet up in nearby towns for quality time together.

If you thought Lottie was steadfast in her search for Frank, then learning about her calm demeanor in the midst of chaos won't throw you for a loop. One of the most famous stories associated with her name comes from a fight between two gamblers that resulted in gunshots and left both men dead. While everyone ran out of the bar once the shots rang out, Lottie stayed behind. When Sheriff Cruger, who had encountered the fight and shot the men involved, expressed disbelief that she had remained in the bar, Lottie had a simple explanation: "You've never been a desperate woman, Sheriff."[1] She stayed to win the hand she had set out to play, more fearful of being poor than losing her life.

Before Lottie and Frank married, she relocated to Kingston, New Mexico, in 1878, where Frank was waiting for her. Together they opened their own gaming room in the Victorio Hotel, as well as a saloon in Silver City. At the time, this region was roaring with wealth from active silver and gold mines—people had money to spend and they were looking for a fun way to do it. The couple also owned a few mines, which they had won in bets, and had a stake in the mines' findings. Their success allowed them to continue pumping money into personal projects—restaurants, two saloons, a hotel, as well as charity work—all while Lottie kept dealing cards at night. It wasn't until a rogue outburst on one of her shifts ended in Frank stabbing and killing *another* disorderly patron that Lottie decided to step away from card playing. The gambler, Dan Baxter, had thrown a billiard ball at Frank, resulting in Frank's violent reaction. (For the record,

Frank was given an out on this one, as it was decided that he had acted in self-defense.)

Lottie spent the rest of her life as a respected member of the community in Kingston. She even founded a bridge club that still exists today: the Golden Gossip Club. Frank died from cancer in 1908 after being with Lottie for more than forty years. Lottie wouldn't meet her own fate for another twenty-six years, on February 9, 1934, at the ripe old age of eighty-nine.

"POKER ALICE" TUBBS

The DEALER in the LATEST FASHIONS, NEVER NOT SMOKING a CIGAR

Alice Tubbs's early life could not have been more different from her adult years. Born in Sudbury, England, in February 1851, Alice was raised by a schoolmaster and his wife; not much is officially known about Alice's mother, aside from her occupation as a housewife, which was common at the time. The family eventually relocated to Virginia and later to Colorado, where Alice would spend the majority of her life, and it was there that she received the best education available to her as an upper-class woman at the time. It was also in Colorado that she met the first of her three husbands, a mining engineer named Frank Duffield.

The couple married around 1870, when Alice was approximately nineteen years old, and moved from the eastern United States to Lake City, Colorado, where Frank was working at the time. Mining was an incredibly dangerous career, and many mines were filled with desperate workers. While working, it wasn't uncommon for miners to fall victim to spontaneous explosions, slips, electrocutions, or mercury poisoning, and unfortunately, that is exactly the kind of fate that befell Frank when, around 1876, an issue with a dynamite charge caused an explosion in the mines and took his life.

When Alice and Frank had first moved to the city, she took up gambling (as a pastime) and had a special affinity for poker. Gambling halls were a big part of life in the Wild West in the late 1800s, but it wasn't often that you saw women frequenting the dens. Alice, however, was known to smoke cigars and carry a gun with her at all times, two other characteristics that certainly weren't considered feminine at the time. After Frank died, Alice's gambling hobby became more of a career—so much so that she earned the moniker "Poker Alice."

She became a poker dealer, and her knack for the game led her to an even bigger audience of gamblers in Buena Vista, Colorado. From there, she made a move to Leadville, Colorado, where there were plenty of miners and gambling halls for Alice to work in. In Leadville, Alice also became known for her now iconic poker face. In the late 1800s, women were expected to greet others with a smile, and this expectation extended to the small group of women who frequented gambling dens. Alice's method, however, was to bring a cigar with her to every hand dealt. She was a master of deception; it was near impossible to decipher any kind of emotion on her face. It was the perfect defense: a blank face that shared no secrets of the cards in front of her.

The crowd of gamblers eventually dried up in Leadville in the mid-1880s, and Alice decided to follow the miners and make her way to Central City, Colorado. When she wasn't working as a dealer, she was out perfecting her own game and joining games with those to whom she often dealt cards. This wasn't the last stop Alice made on her career-growing journey, though. The list of cities she graced with her quick hand only grew: Georgetown, Alamosa, and Silver Plume in Colorado, as well as a supposed stint on the island of Trinidad. Legend has it that she met other women dominating gambling dens during this time, including Eleanor "Madame Moustache" Dumont (whom you can read more about on page 29). While there is no official record of the two women gambling together or forming a friendship, it brings about an incredible visual of these powerful women, dripping with character, going head-to-head in person.

In 1891, Alice found herself in Creede, Colorado, a city responding to the boom in miners with ample gambling dens—and overflow that spilled into the streets in the form of tables set up for gaming. Here, you couldn't escape the game of poker. At the same time, the addition of a railroad station in Creede benefitted the surrounding towns. One of these nearby cities, called Bachelor, became just as popular, quickly matching the size of Creede, and Alice traveled there often. She made friends like Soapy Smith, a local crime boss known for showcasing (and making a lot of money from) a hoax called the "petrified man"—he charged 10 cents a head to view what was actually a skeleton covered in cement. Alice also became close with a saloon owner and card dealer named Robert Ford, better known as the man who shot and killed Jesse James. Alice later saw a friend of Jesse's shoot Robert inside his own saloon.

Alice only moved on after a fire ravaged the majority of Creede in 1892. She found herself hunting for a home outside Colorado for the first time in her adult life, specifically in Deadwood, South Dakota. Deadwood may sound familiar to you if you're a fan of classic American road trips, Wild West history, or western movies. It was this city that gave birth to so many of the legends that make the Wild West such an inspiration for movies, television shows, and books. Deadwood was also far from new—by the time Alice got there, it had served as a hub of activity for miners, gamblers, and more for close to a decade. But it was in this city, bustling with activity, that Alice met her second love: Warren Tubbs, a local house painter who also gambled for fun. Together, they would travel all over the country to play poker.

By this time, Alice's name would perk up a few ears across the Wild West. But it was a trip to Silver City, New Mexico, that made her famous. On this adventure, Alice won $6,000 playing poker, which would be worth nearly $170,000 today. In true Alice fashion, she used some of her winnings to further her career as a dealer in Deadwood, which involved visiting New York to go dress shopping. Ask Alice in person, and she would most likely claim this was a business expense, as donning the latest styles served as an added distraction for her opponents.

The couple bought a home outside Deadwood, and all was well for years. But their collective journey ended in 1909, when Warren died, leaving Alice a widow once again. A change in social atmosphere eventually pushed her out of Deadwood, as the Wild West was quickly being repopulated with more modern characters who lacked the criminal records of its previous tenants. But Alice stayed in South Dakota, moving to the town of Sturgis, where she opened a small gambling den that doubled as her home and named it Poker's Palace. She also employed a number of women in her den, something that still wasn't popular in the early 1900s.

In 1913, on a day she was managing her den and accommodating a batch of soldiers visiting the area, the crowd of patrons quickly became too much for her small space to handle, and people began to vandalize the home, cutting the electrical wires and attempting to break into the den. Alice's response was to shoot her gun out the window to thwart the boisterous crew, and unfortunately, a young soldier found himself at the other end of the shot. Alice, who was sixty-two years old at this point, was arrested for murder, tried, found guilty, and sentenced. After she appealed the conviction, she was acquitted on the grounds of justifiable homicide. This was far from the only entry on her criminal record, though. Alice was frequently fined for running a brothel and general acts of drunkenness.

The rest of her years rolled out relatively quietly compared to her travels across the west. She met her third husband, George Huckert, when she was sixty-five years old. They lived together on George's ranch, where he raised sheep, until his death in 1924. Alice's name made the papers once more when Deadwood hosted a parade celebrating its Wild West history in 1925. She was invited to participate in the festivities and the local newspapers began to profile Alice and her peers, bringing them into the limelight once again. Alice lived for another five years before dying after a surgery on February 13, 1930. You can still visit her home in Sturgis, as well as her gravesite at the local Catholic cemetery.

STEPHANIE ST. CLAIR

HARLEM'S "MADAM QUEEN *of* POLICY"

———◆>••<◆———

Those who were familiar with Stephanie St. Clair knew her as a refined, impeccably well-dressed, French-speaking Harlem-based woman with deep connections to the local gangs. And most of that is true. But to really understand Stephanie, you have to know where she came from.

Stephanie was born on December 24, 1897, in Guadeloupe in the Caribbean, before moving to Marseilles, France. In 1911, when she was thirteen years old, Stephanie made her way to New York from

France via steamboat. It's important to note that there are differing opinions about her age here. Some sources claim that she was thirteen when she landed in New York, while others cast her as old as twenty-three. But biographer Shirley Stewart, author of *The World of Stephanie St. Clair: An Entrepreneur, Race Woman and Outlaw in Early Twentieth Century Harlem,* put her at the age of thirteen, which is the most widely accepted angle. All age-related questions aside, once in America, Stephanie put emphasis on her supposed time in France rather than her birthplace in the Caribbean (where her community also spoke French), and it was this branding that helped elevate her in Harlem society. She dressed in the latest fashions, spoke perfect French, and was well-educated. But for as put-together as she seemed, she had one thing working against her: a quick, and ferocious, temper.

It wasn't long before Stephanie stepped into a leading role in the Forty Thieves gang, who mainly focused on theft and extortion. During her involvement with this gang, she helped develop a numbers racket by investing $10,000 of her own money. The contribution earned her the title of "policy banker"—and spawned a number of her nicknames as well, including "Madam Queen of Policy." But Stephanie's title also put her on people's radars, notably mobsters looking to take stakes in new revenue streams.

Up until 1930, Stephanie successfully ran her numbers rackets in Harlem with her partner—a well-known mobster by the name of Ellsworth "Bumpy" Johnson. At this point, more mob members were starting up their own numbers rackets, too, which created new rivalries for the pair. Their largest competition was Dutch Schultz, a violence-prone mob boss. Slowly and surely, Dutch's business affected Stephanie and Ellsworth's endeavors.

When the mid-1930s came around, Stephanie was changed. She was no longer partnered (in life or business) with Ellsworth. She handed over her racket to Dutch and another mobster with a numbers racket named Charles "Lucky" Luciano. Officially out of the business, Stephanie took her attentions elsewhere, and I'm willing to bet you'd never guess the turn that comes next.

With Ellsworth in her rearview mirror, Stephanie met and fell in love with Sufi Abdul Hamid (born Eugene Brown), the leader of an Islamic-Buddhist cult. In addition to claiming to be a descendant of Egyptian pharaohs, Abdul was an open anti-Semite. He had a history of crime himself, having been convicted of stabbing a communist rally organizer in 1936. Despite Abdul's work and prejudices, though, Stephanie was an activist who tirelessly advocated for the rights of Black people by writing letters to editors of Black-owned magazines and newspapers. Talk about an unlikely pair.

But Stephanie's relationship with Abdul had a rough ending. On his way to see a lawyer in January 1938, he was shot. An all-white jury believed Stephanie had committed the crime—and she was sentenced to at least two years in prison. Once released, she continued fighting for civil and economic rights for Black people. Though she never (officially) committed another crime, many believe she was protected by her ex-partner, Ellsworth, up until his death in 1968. Protected or not, Stephanie died in 1969 at the age of eighty-two.

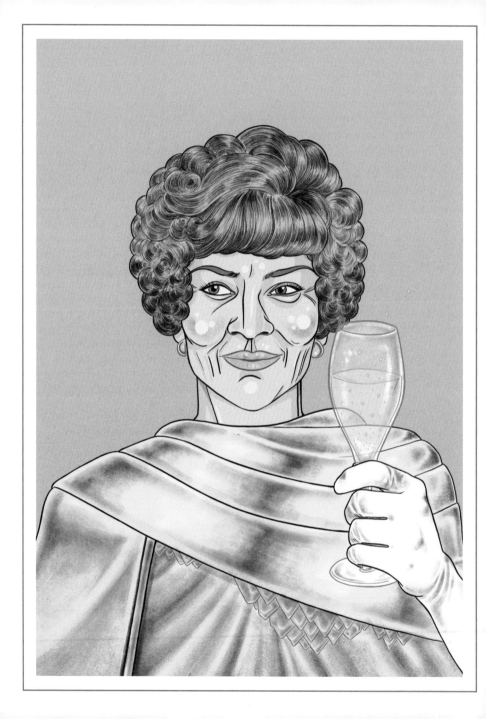

JUDY BAYLEY

The FIRST LADY of GAMBLING

I want to start off this bio by being completely clear on one thing: Judy Bayley sounds like an absolute delight. Although this book features plenty of grisly murder, ghastly crime, and bad blood, I also wanted to spotlight a few women whose impressive accomplishments outshine any illegal activities or unladylike professions in which they may have been involved. Judy Bayley is one of those women. She stepped into a field dominated by men and challenged societal expectations for a woman at the time by owning and operating a gambling empire in the most famous gambling hub in the United States.

Born in Dallas, Texas, in 1915, Judy was the daughter of Fred and Ada Belk. She had an active childhood and showed a clear talent for performing, specifically as a dancer. After graduating with degrees in English and music from Southern Methodist University, Judy met and married Warren "Doc" Bayley, who owned and operated a chain of hotels throughout California. In 1953, the couple moved to Las Vegas to take advantage of the booming resort and casino business in the area. In 1956 they opened the Hacienda Hotel, and its casino addition followed a year later. Warren ran the business—which makes sense, given his experience in the industry. But when he unexpectedly died of a heart attack in 1964, Judy took over ownership of the hotel and casino, despite having never operated a business, let alone a hotel, in her life.

Judy became the first woman in Nevada's state history to be the sole owner-operator of a hotel-casino. She had her work cut out for her, as Warren had driven the business into decline by the time of his death, but Judy's tendency to entertain was a big pull in her strategy as a business owner. She was incredibly hands-on, interacting with the staff on all levels, introducing new games like keno and poker to the gaming floor, and keeping a spotlight on the establishment in the media. Her kindness, attention to detail, and empathy toward her employees kept people around and created a sense of loyalty that wasn't commonly found in uber-competitive Las Vegas business.

Aside from providing a good place for her employees to work, Judy was also a philanthropist, donating her time and money to fight terminal diseases and better the lives of children. She utilized her successful business to host a number of fund-raisers, starting with the first Heart Fund Telethon, in January 1968. She also founded the Hacienda Trail Ride, which was a fund-raiser for a slew of charities, including the American Cancer Society. As the University of Las Vegas (UNLV) ramped up its growth, Judy readily provided funds for various projects. The last donation she gave before dying on December 31, 1971, was a $65,000 contribution to finance a new performing arts center for UNLV. Naturally, the theater was named after her, and was completed soon after her death.

Judy owned a casino at a very different time and in a very different political climate than many of the other female gamblers featured in this book. But the one thing that links her to them is that she, too, refused to conform to the traditional gender role women during her time were expected to fulfill. Being an entrepreneurial woman in a largely male-dominated industry must have come with its challenges. In fact, Judy may have had an even stronger will than most of her peers, given her squeaky-clean reputation.

So, let's toast this lady who seemed to do it right.

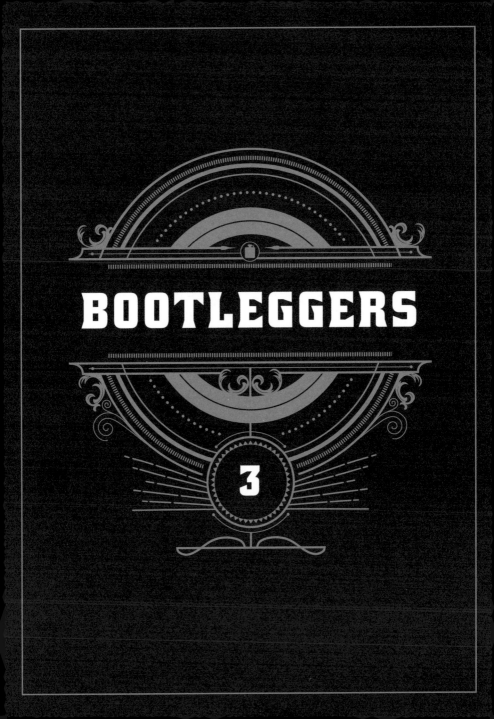

BOOTLEGGERS

3

THE GALS OF GRAIN ALCOHOL

I n the 1920s, people across the United States were in a tizzy over Prohibition and the anti-liquor laws that came with it—so they decided to risk massive fines and jail time to keep the party going. Prohibition made it illegal to sell alcohol anywhere in the United States, but this led to the increased popularity of a practice called bootlegging. Bootlegging was a well-known activity and became particularly popular in the Midwest in the 1880s, when people began smuggling alcohol in flasks during trades with the Native Americans. The term was brought back into the spotlight when Prohibition swept the nation.

However, being a bootlegger was incredibly dangerous. Not only was moonshine, the general name given to the alcohol bootleggers produced, highly inconsistent and potentially deadly to drink, the sale of it could land you in jail. When Prohibition was first introduced, bootleggers began smuggling alcohol from places like Canada and Mexico into the United States. When the borders became tighter and it became tougher to continue this activity, bootleggers began making their own alcohol or sourcing it from other Americans who were distilling it.

A majority of the time, you'll hear about the men who made their mark on the history of bootlegging. There are two reasons for this: 1) There were a whole lot of men risking this kind of danger to make some money (and to have booze for their own recreational activities); and 2) The women who took to bootlegging had often fallen on desperate times and were bootlegging in order to provide for their families. The public held a general sense of empathy toward this group of women, which often worked to their advantage if they were ever brought to court, as was the case with Maggie Bailey, a kindhearted queen of small talk whom you will learn more about in this section. Also important to remember is that bootlegging required all types of people to make it work. In other words, these lawbreaking ladies proved that being a successful bootlegger was not just about mixing, transporting, and selling the alcohol.

Terms to Know

Rumrunning: Another popular term for bootlegging, more often associated with the transportation of alcohol across city and state lines.

Prohibition: The period of time between 1920 and 1933 when the sale of alcohol was illegal in the United States.

Moonshine: Alcohol that was made illegally or smuggled illegally.

Rotgut: Liquor that was poorly made and of poor quality, often toxic.

Hooch: Alcoholic liquor, specifically referring to liquor that was made illegally.

Volstead Act: A US law enacted in 1919 that made the manufacture and sale of alcoholic beverages illegal.

MARY LOUISE CECILIA "TEXAS" GUINAN

QUEEN *of the* SPEAKEASIES

⬥⬥⬥

Search for the name "Mary Louise Cecilia" online and you'll likely receive a list of results referencing an actress first. Dig a little deeper, and you'll see some mentions of a Prohibition-era nightclub hostess. Fun fact: These results all refer to the same person.

Mary Louise Cecilia Guinan—who came to be known as "Texas" Guinan—was born in Waco, Texas, but made her way to New York City in 1905. There, she built up her acting résumé with roles in productions like *The Gay Musician*, *Miss Bob White*, and *The Hoyden*. But it was an entirely different performance that caught the eye of her eventual husband, bootlegger and racketeer Larry Fay.

One night in New York City in 1924, Mary was playing the role of mistress of ceremonies at the after-party for a show at New York's Winter Garden. Her boisterous personality inspired Larry to offer her a job as hostess and mistress of ceremonies at his El Fay Club, an infamous speakeasy on Forty-Seventh Street, near Broadway in Manhattan. Mary would sit on a stool at the center of the club, whistle in hand, and greet all those who passed in her roaring voice. Her favorite salutation to yell at all who entered was "Hello, sucker!" although when it came to a rich out-of-towner, she preferred "Big Butter-and-Egg Man." She was great for business. But for all the yelling and commotion I'm painting a picture of, remember: This was an illegal speakeasy. Finding the club and getting in were no easy feat. El Fay Club was only open between midnight and five a.m. and was located at the top of a flight of stairs, behind a door with a peephole. Inside, the space fit no more than eighty people at a time. There was a small stage where you would often find acts ranging from tap dancers to chorus lines. According to the Mob Museum, the nightclub's guests even included Babe Ruth, Charles Lindbergh, Gloria Swanson, Charlie Chaplin, Prince Edward, and Clara Bow.

Eventually, the police shut down El Fay Club for serving alcohol, but Mary and Larry wasted no time in finding a new space for their patrons, on Forty-Fifth Street, just two blocks from their previous establishment. Frequent police raids landed Mary in many newspaper headlines, and with her newfound celebrity, she was ready to take on her own endeavor. Larry wasn't as convinced, given that Mary was his biggest attraction for the club. Sensing his dependence, Mary hired some muscle to put Larry in his place, a message he eventually gave in to. At the end of it all, she did end up opening her own place: the 300 Club, on West Fifty-Fourth Street. She was arrested for a suspected Volstead violation in 1927, but because it was never proven that she had any ownership of the speakeasy, she pleaded guilty to simply being the venue's hostess.

After she opened the 300 Club, she also began performing again in her own revue, called *Padlocks of 1927*. From there, she even produced two movies: *Queen of the Night Clubs* and *Broadway Thru a Keyhole*. All the while, she kept her signature sense of humor. When her revue company didn't pick up popularity overseas (notably in France), she changed the revue's name to *Too Hot for Paris*.

On November 5, 1933, the speakeasy world said goodbye to Mary. She had fallen ill the previous day while on tour in Vancouver due to undiagnosed ulcerative colitis; the condition required surgery, which she did not survive. She died one month after Prohibition had ended. All in all, it's no surprise that more than 12,000 people attended her funeral in New York, suckers and big butter-and-egg men included.

WILLIE CARTER SHARPE

The SPEEDSTER *with* DIAMONDS
in HER TEETH

———❖❯••❮❖———

I n the 1930s, Virginia's Franklin County was the center of a Prohibition-era trial that would go down in history. The reason for the trial was a common crime of the time: transporting illegally made alcohol (also known as "bootlegging," as you now well know). One of the leading causes for this regional shift to black-market commerce was the arrival, at the turn of the century, of the chestnut blight, a parasitic fungus that attacked and killed American chestnut trees (*Castanea dentata*) and quickly destroyed nearly the entire species. For generations, families had lived off money made from their chestnut crops—both from lumber for building and furniture-making and from the chestnuts themselves—and many of the same families who had relied on the trees to make their living turned to bootlegging to get by.

According to a 2018 article in the *Richmond Times-Dispatch* titled "'The Wettest Place on Earth': Moonshine, a Virginia County and a Trial that Captivated the Nation," there was enough booze coming out of this rural region in Virginia to warrant an investigation that resulted in the Great Moonshine Conspiracy Trial, which involved more than 289 people (defendants, witnesses, and coconspirators combined). To give you an idea of the production hauls, "nearly 34 million pounds (of sugar, an ingredient used in making moonshine) were sold in the county during those four years, which works out to an annualized consumption of 354 pounds for each man, woman and child," according to Sherwood Anderson, an author hired by *Liberty* magazine to write an account of the trial.

During this time, there were those who made the moonshine and those who transported it—arguably a more dangerous gig, if you consider the mass amount of alcohol being distributed from this geographically small region and how much easier it would have been to get caught. At the center of this activity was the thirtysomething Willie Carter Sharpe, a transporter known for her adventurous driving and diamond-studded teeth. Her job was much more complicated than getting the product from point A to point B, though. Police officers in the county were making money accepting protection bribes from bootleggers, which was a tricky situation to navigate while making the sales and drop-offs. This wasn't little-known information, either; every level of law enforcement hierarchy was involved in the spiderweb of bribes, and it expanded to neighboring counties as well. In January 1931, a document covering all crime and law enforcement while outlining the effects of Prohibition published by the Wickersham Commission characterized Franklin County to FBI chief J. Edgar Hoover as the "wettest county on Earth." An intimate investigation followed, eventually prompting the Great Moonshine Conspiracy Trial.

Amid all this high-profile action, Willie was transporting liquor across the Virginia state border, and she quickly became known as the "Rumrunning Queen" for her frequent close-call escapes. Between the years of 1926 and 1931, Willie was making and selling her own moonshine, and delivered an estimated 220,000 gallons of moonshine to her buyers in that time. The most visually delightful part of all this is that Willie drove a souped-up muscle car, according to "Moonshining in Franklin County: The Tales They Told; The Legacy They Left," a 2016 article in the *Franklin News-Post*. And she was innovative: To get overloaded vehicles up steep hills, she and her colleagues would hook the cars up to one another, back bumper to front bumper, until they all made it safely to the top. It was not an easy, quiet, or quick process. If the cops ever wised up to her scheme, Willie would fire up the engine on her muscle car and lead the officers on a high-speed chase to divert their attention away from her colleagues.

The cars used to transport moonshine also came with a few souped-up additions of their own. In an effort to hide the extra loads from the police, some cars had a built-in second gas tank made just for storing alcohol. Others had extra-strong springs around the wheels to keep the extra weight from pulling the car body lower on the hubs. And the really fun cars had a set of hand brakes that only controlled the back set of wheels, allowing the driver to spin the vehicle and change directions with the pull of a handle.

Eventually, though, Willie was caught, and at her trial, she professed, "It was the excitement that got me . . . Cars skattering, dashing along the streets." Willie was found guilty and did her time at the Alderson federal prison (the very same place Martha Stewart would serve her own sentence seventy-three years later). After she was released, Willie alleged she received letters from high-society women asking her to give them a taste of her speedy skills on a personal drive.[1] Whether that's true or not, I do love visualizing these fancy women letting their hair down and joyriding with Willie.

MAGGIE BAILEY

The QUEEN of MOUNTAIN BOOTLEGGERS

If you spotted Maggie Bailey walking down the sidewalk, she would be the last person you'd expect to be involved in illegal activity. In fact, she would most likely have reminded you of someone's grandmother. And that first impression would ring true in some aspects—she was an older woman and a kind individual, always looking to help those who were less fortunate and take care of others. But she also sold booze out of her kitchen well into her old age.

Maggie lived in a place called Clovertown in Kentucky's Harlan County. Something important to keep in mind is that selling alcohol in this particular town is still illegal, nearly one hundred years after the repeal of Prohibition: Harlan is a dry county, meaning it's against the law to sell any alcoholic beverage within county lines. Maggie was prosecuted for making and selling moonshine only once, in the 1940s, for which she served eighteen months in a federal prison, but she continued to sell alcohol from her home until her death in 2005.

Maggie was a huge part of the Clovertown community. As opposed to the chaotic scenes you may have conjured up in your brain for what buying moonshine must have been like during Prohibition, buying alcohol at Maggie's was akin to visiting a family friend. In an interview with NPR's *All Things Considered,* her lawyer and good friend Otis Doan shared that Maggie would want to start a conversation with anyone who came her way, and would remember most faces that showed up. It was a simple process: You would come to her home, indulge in some small talk, and tell Maggie what you were looking to buy; she would bring it out, you would pay, and then you'd be on your way.[1] There were no car chases and no rowdy patrons. Otis shared that there were only two types of people she wouldn't sell to: children and, as Maggie put it, "drunkards." She herself did not even drink.

One of the main reasons Maggie was convicted only once, according to Otis, was that she was such a supportive member of the community.[2] She helped local children make their way through college by contributing to their tuition. She would show up with food for families who were struggling through rough times. She helped her sister, Lobella, raise her two sons. Combine that with the fact that she entered the courtroom in her signature dress and apron, topped with a grandmotherly head of gray hair, and you can imagine why people were hesitant to continue prosecuting such a beloved resident.

Her nickname, "The Queen of Mountain Bootleggers," would have you believe that Maggie was a scary, gun-toting woman warding off deals gone wrong at every turn. But that could not be further from the truth. In fact, I'd wager that her motivation for keeping up her business would put a smile on your face: "She said it kept her alive," Otis shared with NPR. "She said it kept her young." And it did—at the time of her death on December 3, 2005, Maggie was 101 years old.[3]

MARY WAZENIAK

The FIRST WOMAN CONVICTED for SERVING POISONED LIQUOR

———◆≻••≺◆———

You may think making and slinging moonshine was all car chases and drunken fun, but it came with its fair share of tragedy, too. The story of Mary Wazeniak is especially dark. She turned her home in La Grange Park, Illinois, into a saloon that welcomed all sorts of characters. Mary's operation was relatively quiet, if the lack of headlines and folklore (compared to other moonshiners) is any indication. But one night in 1923 completely turned her life upside down.

Something to know about the process of making moonshine is that it was often far from scientific. The ingredients being used in the early twentieth century were usually never precisely measured and the workspaces were unkempt and unclean. Both of those points aside, the ingredients themselves varied widely. It was tough for bootleggers in the 1900s to know exactly how strong the alcohol had become—let alone what it was made of—which resulted in some pretty devastating effects. Pure methanol was one of those dangerous ingredients, and Mary used it in her mix, which gave her moonshine a potent kick.

In 1923, a man named George L. Rheaton and three of his friends visited Mary. After taking a handful of her 15-cent shots—there are different accounts out there, but most suggest he took five or six—he made his way out of her saloon and dropped dead a couple hundred feet from the front door.

An autopsy found that George had died of methanol poisoning, which led to Mary being the very first woman to be convicted for selling poisoned liquor in Illinois. An investigation of Mary's moonshine later confirmed the ingredient: Her hooch showed traces of wood alcohol, another name for methanol because of the fact that it was often distilled using wood. In smaller doses, or as little as 10 milliliters of the pure ingredient, methanol can cause blindness. Talk about risky business. Once convicted, Mary—who became known as "Moonshine Mary"—received a prison sentence of one year to life.

GLORIA DE CASARES

The SCOTCH QUEEN of the SEAS

———◆≫••≪◆———

A lot of bootlegging and moonshine production occurring in the United States during Prohibition affected lands far from its borders. During this time, most commerce involved a significant amount of shipping, which was a major opportunity for particularly crafty importers to provide Americans with foreign liquors. Gloria de Casares, the wife of a very wealthy Argentinean man, was one of these importers.

She snagged her biggest headline in 1925, after one of her ships en route to the United States from London was seized and ten thousand cases of scotch were discovered on board. The ship's captain gave the police Gloria's name while he was being questioned, and she took the fall. As a result, Gloria was never able to enter any United States harbor again without being questioned by the authorities to make sure she wasn't bringing in illegal goods to sell. On one occasion, Gloria was confined to a hotel room and questioned by British authorities. The police also confiscated any clothing she had with her valuing more than $25. Gloria shared her displeasure with the *New York Times*: "What am I to do? First I am deprived of my nationality. Now they want to deprive me of all my clothes over $25 worth. Twenty-five dollars is just about enough for a hat. Do they expect a woman to go about the world with $25 worth of clothing?"[1]

After all this trouble, Gloria never once gave in and admitted to bootlegging, but she did run into trouble with Ellis Island immigration authorities in April 1927, which put a damper on her business.

According to an article entitled "Overstays Her Leave Here: Mrs. De Casares, 'Queen of Bootleggers,' Forfeits $500 Bond":

> *Mrs. de Casares, an Englishwoman who married an Argentine doctor, thus becoming a subject of Argentina, arrived in New York on April 18 following her deportation from England because she was the owner of a rum-running yacht named* General Serret, *which caused her to be dubbed "Queen of the Bootleggers" in the London newspapers. She had a French visa on her passport, but no visa to enter the United States. The young woman told the immigration officials that while she was the owner of the* General Serret, *she had not known to what use it had been put.*[2]

And her excuse worked. She was granted fifteen days in the United States, as well as a bond of $500. She did receive one extension, but a warrant for her arrest and deportation was eventually issued.

Unfortunately, you'll be hard-pressed to find out what became of Gloria after 1927. One can imagine that being deported from two countries that were key to her success as a bootlegger couldn't have been good for business.

STELLA BELOUMANT

The BOOTLEGGER TAKEN DOWN AFTER a 24-HOUR STAKEOUT

——◆❥••❦◆——

Stella Beloumant, like many of us, had a soft spot for wine. She ran her own bootlegging ring—one of the largest during Prohibition—in Elko, Nevada. Stella was so well-known, she was targeted by the entire Prohibition enforcement task force before being taken down in 1926.

What's most interesting about Stella's situation is the amount of federal attention it received. During Prohibition, it was often hard to nail women for this particular crime. More often than not, they were given the benefit of the doubt for being the "fairer sex"—i.e., juries often found it hard to believe that women could commit such crimes. Fred Minnick's book *Whiskey Women* puts it best: "It was difficult for church-going America to comprehend mothers and grandmas strapping flasks to their inner thighs or toting revolvers to protect a truck full of hooch. Prohibitionists wanted citizens to believe good women made apple pie and tucked their children in bed at night."[1]

It took a twenty-four-hour stakeout involving two dry agents—a name given to Prohibition agents who shut down illegal alcohol productions—a district attorney, a squad of sheriff's deputies, and the number two official for the Bureau of Prohibition to put a stop to Stella's operation. Even more impressive than the number of people on her tail might have been what they seized that night: 820 gallons of her wine. To give you some perspective, that equates to 4,140 bottles of the wine you're used to seeing on the dinner table.

Although she may have been taken down, she will forever be known as the woman who was producing more wine than some French wineries at the time.

JOSEPHINE DOODY

The BOOTLEG LADY *of* GLACIER PARK

———◆>••<◆———

I f anyone in this book deserves to have a movie made about her, it might just be Josephine Doody. Most of her story takes place in Montana's Glacier National Park, but legend has it that she got there after killing a man at a dance hall in Colorado (she claimed self-defense). After being on the run from the police, she eventually landed in McCarthyville, Montana, a rough mining settlement on Marias Pass, where she hunkered down and sadly developed a dangerous opium addiction. If it weren't for a national park ranger named Dan Doody (yes, that was his actual name), Josephine would likely have had a very different fate.

Dan kidnapped Josephine and brought her to his own home, a remote cabin on the Middle Fork of the Flathead River, so she could recover and make her way back into sobriety. While there are no details regarding that time in Josephine's life, you can imagine the hardships that must have come with going through withdrawal, combined with the disorienting company of a stranger and a new environment, but eventually Josephine did get better, and she and Dan got married.

It was on this property, located in what is now Glacier National

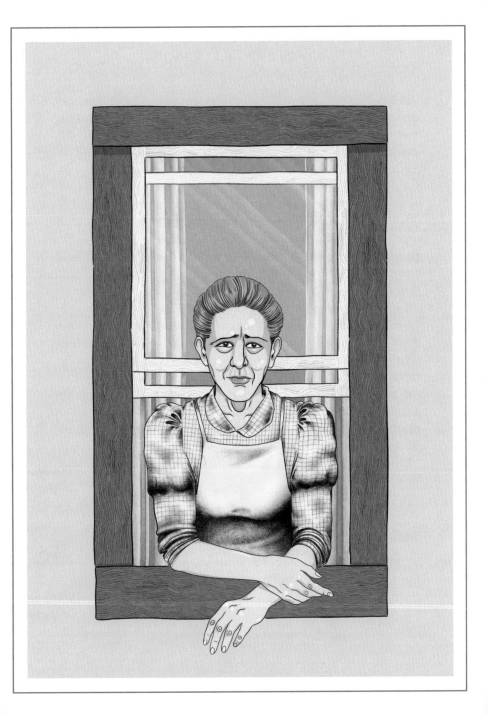

Park, that Josephine and Dan survived—hunting, trapping furs, and chasing mountain lions together. Oh, and it was there that they created their own moonshine still as well. Josephine organized an entire operation on the 160-acre property, including a special way of placing and filling orders for passengers traveling on the trains that stopped nearby. To place an order, the train conductor would toot the whistle one time for each gallon of moonshine passengers wished to purchase. From there, Josephine would gather the moonshine, load it into a small boat, and float it across the river.

When the national park began to expand, eventually taking over Josephine and Dan's property, there were new worries for the still: How would the pair keep park rangers unaware of their business? On top of that, Dan lost his job as a ranger in 1916 after being accused of excessive poaching of the park's wildlife. When he died five years later in 1921, Josephine was left to keep the business rolling. Although she continued to make moonshine, she also turned the log cabin she had owned with Dan into a hunting and fishing lodge as a way of making ends meet.

After a while, Josephine became close friends with another ranger, Clyde Fauley Sr., who oversaw the park's Nyack region, where her lodge was located. This was now late into Prohibition, around 1929 or 1930, according to Clyde's son. "She would have been about 78 at the time," Clyde shared in a 2012 article titled "Doody Homestead Housed 'Bootleg Lady of Glacier Park'" in the *Missoulian*:

> She was right on the trail and at that time rangers
> patrolled constantly, in the winter on snowshoes and
> in the summer on foot. They didn't just sit in the pickup
> and play cop. They patrolled. And her cabin was
> right at the intersection of the Boundary Trail and the
> Harrison Lake Trail. She made sure my dad had pie and
> coffee every time he stopped. She was a pretty mild-

mannered old lady by then, but of course still had her ideas and opinions.[1]

Soon after Thanksgiving 1930, Josephine moved to Deerlick Creek, just across the river from her cabin, according to Clyde. Author John Fraley may know the most about her life, as outlined in his book *Wild River Pioneers: Adventures in the Middle Fork of the Flathead, Great Bear Wilderness, and Glacier National Park.* He was able to trace her beginning to Macon County, Georgia, confirming that she had indeed lived in Colorado and worked as a dance hall girl at one point. John also found her death certificate, which noted that Josephine died of pneumonia in January 1936. At the time of her death, she had been living with another man, Charlie Holland, at her home in Deerlick Creek. When she fell ill, Charlie put her on a train—against Josephine's wishes—to a hospital in Kalispell, Montana, where she died. A small funeral was held; few of her friends attended and Charlie never showed up. It was also noted that her iconic gold-nugget earrings were missing—a hint that Charlie may not have been the best friend to have for her last living months.

You can still visit the cabin Josephine and Dan lived in at Glacier National Park.

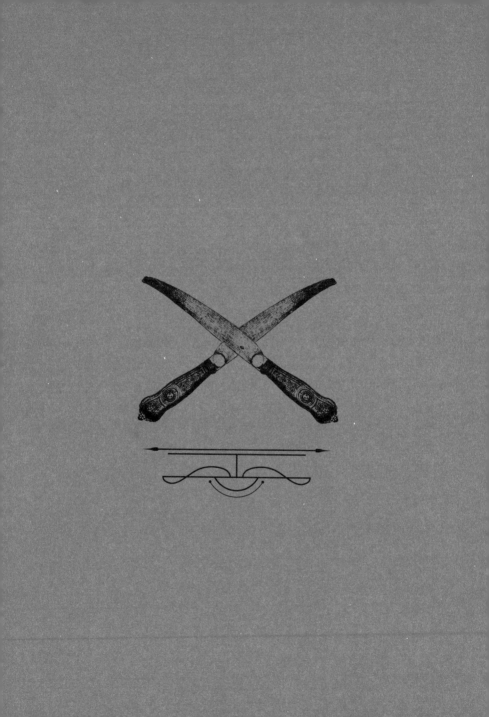

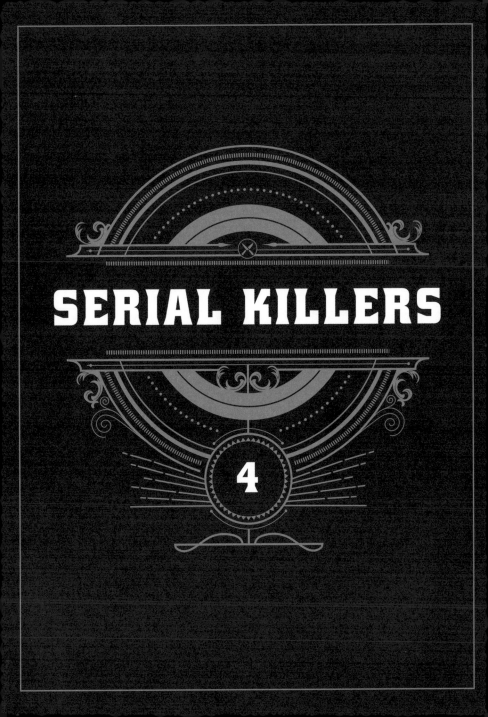

SERIAL KILLERS

4

LADIES WHO WERE LETHAL

It's common to hear the phrase "serial killer" and immediately think of a man. Some of the most notorious serial killers were men. Their lives and crimes have inspired countless movie scripts and docuseries—and continue to do so today. As a result, we tend not to discuss female serial killers as often, but in this section, you'll learn about some of the most infamous female serial killers of yore.

As Ann Jones suggests in her 1980 book *Women Who Kill*, society has long feared women who rebel against expectations for them to be docile wives and daughters. But as you may have guessed, since this is a book all about lawbreaking ladies, the particular women in this section were not exactly what many would consider to be feminist icons. They were, to put it mildly, downright dangerous.

Terms to Know

Multimurderer: Another word for serial killer that refers to anyone who has murdered more than one person.

Serial killer: A person who has committed a series of murders and often follows a predictable pattern of behavior leading up to, during, and after the killings.

Sadist: A person who experiences pleasure from inflicting pain or humiliation upon another person.

Signature: An identifying mark left behind by a serial killer.

Mask of sanity: An attempt to reinterpret the so-called psychopathic personality; when a killer appears to be trustworthy or caring but they're hiding their true intentions.

Angel of death: A criminal who targets people whom they are directly responsible for taking care of, intentionally harming or killing them instead.

ELIZABETH BÁTHORY

The BLOOD COUNTESS

———◆>••<◆———

The many, many crimes of Elizabeth Báthory are . . . gruesome, to say the least. This serial killer has been named one of history's most prolific, according to Guinness World Records, and her story is more akin to the plot of a horror movie than anything you think could happen in real life. The most brief description of it is: Elizabeth was a vampire.

One thing to note about Elizabeth's life is that much of it has been sensationalized. She was born in 1560, and since then people have spent hundreds of years fictionalizing her acts, making it very difficult to know the exact truth. So please take the following tale with a grain of salt.

Elizabeth was born into Hungarian nobility. By the age of eleven, she was betrothed to Ferencz Nádasdy, a member of another prominent Hungarian family, but during their engagement, Elizabeth became pregnant with another man's baby. The father of her child was of a lower social rank, and when Ferencz discovered him, he subjected the man to a horrific death by castration . . . before siccing his dogs on the man to finish the job. Eventually, though, Ferencz went through with his marriage to Elizabeth in 1575, and her child was hidden from the public.

As a soldier, Ferencz traveled often, and Elizabeth would keep busy while he was away, finding lovers in her husband's family's various castles around Hungary, including Castle Čachtice. Over the course of their marriage, Elizabeth bore Ferencz four children, and she remained his wife until his death in 1604.

Plagued by the beauty she was born with, Elizabeth fought to maintain her looks after becoming a mother, and she believed that the best way to do this was by ingesting the blood of young women.

I'll give you a moment to let that sink in—although unfortunately, it gets worse. It wasn't long before the rumor mill kicked into high gear and news of her sadistic hobby spread. According to legend, Elizabeth would take the lives of her servants and other young women who were sent to her under the guise of attending a manners school of sorts. Alleged witnesses of Elizabeth's crimes claimed her methods of torturing these women before drinking their blood included starving, cutting, biting, and beating them and sticking needles into various parts of their bodies, like their lips. Some women were even burned with irons or metal coins.

The rumors became so rampant that in 1610, six years after her husband's death, a Lutheran minister reported Elizabeth to the authorities. During the investigation into her crimes, four of Elizabeth's closest servants were also found guilty—and paid a price for their involvement. Three of them were immediately executed, while the other was imprisoned for life. Elizabeth, on the other hand, spent the rest of her years in solitary confinement in a room without windows in Castle Čachtice. She died in that room in 1614, at the age of fifty-four.

GIULIA TOFANA

The COSMETICS KILLER

—❧••❦—

If there was ever a person you could deem a "professional poisoner," Giulia Tofana would be your gal. Her motive and process for killing were entirely different from those of the other women you'll find in this section, too, as Giulia's goal was ultimately to free women from their unhappy marriages. However, the way she went about this may make you never want to touch your makeup again.

In the mid-1600s, Giulia started a cosmetics line called Aqua Tofana, which was sold throughout Southern Italy. During this period, arranged marriages were what brought many couples together, and the idea of divorce was not only unheard of, but illegal. As a result, many women suffered through abusive relationships with no way out of their unions—until either husband or wife died, of course. But this is where Giulia's product comes into play: Aqua Tofana was actually packed with poison—specifically arsenic, lead, and belladonna.

For fifty years, Giulia was able to fool the authorities and sell her poisoned cosmetics. Women throughout the region increasingly became aware of her makeup's properties and how they afforded an opportunity to escape bad marriages, if used correctly. And she probably would have continued to get away with it if it hadn't been for one customer who couldn't go through with her crime. As the story goes, after tainting her husband's soup with Aqua Tofana, the woman was filled with regret and stopped him from eating his poisoned dinner, but refused to tell him why. Alarmed at her reaction, he forced a confession out of his wife and turned her over to the police.

From there, she pointed the finger at Giulia, spilling Giulia's secret and putting an end to the operation. Giulia was given a heads-up that she'd been exposed and went to a church to seek sanctuary, which she was granted, but the rumor mill worked against her: Word spread that she had poisoned the water that served all of Rome, and her sanctuary was subsequently revoked. After being turned over to the papal authorities, Giulia was tortured until she admitted her crimes, which amounted to poisoning more than six hundred men between the years of 1633 and 1651. She was found guilty of her crimes, of course, and sentenced to execution, along with her daughter and three of her employees. All were killed in Campo de' Fiori in July of 1659.

However, they weren't the only ones who suffered. Some of the women who purchased Aqua Tofana were also jailed or executed for their hand in the poisonings. The act of poisoning via Aqua Tofana became so well-known that even Mozart, after falling ill in 1791, diagnosed himself as being a victim of the cosmetic poisoning. He said, "I feel definitely that I will not last much longer; I am sure that I have been poisoned." He went on to claim, "Someone has given me Acqua Tofana and calculated the precise time of my death."[1]

In its original iteration, Aqua Tofana was sold in powder form, so that it could be placed on a table without raising suspicion. At one point, it was even available as a liquid in a small vial, disguised as a religious oil. If anything, this story is enough to make you second-guess what's in your makeup . . . or that cool-looking bottle you picked up in an antiques store.

DARYA SALTYKOVA

The NOBLEWOMAN WHO TORTURED and KILLED HER SERFS

———❖••❖———

There are few words to describe just how heinous Darya Saltykova was. An enthusiastic fan of torturing the women closest to her, she was so ruthless you'd be hard-pressed to find a female serial killer more evil.

Born on November 3, 1730, in Moscow, Russia, Darya Saltykova became the poster-woman of her time for abusing serfs, who were agricultural laborers "bound under the feudal system to work on (their) lord's estate," according to the *Oxford English Dictionary*. She was a Russian noblewoman, married to Gleb Saltykov, with whom she had two sons. Gleb died, leaving Darya a widowed mother at the age of twenty-six. Upon his death, she inherited a large property, as well as up to six hundred laborers who worked on the farm, and it was at this time in Darya's life that her sadistic tendencies were unleashed—sadly, at the expense of many lives.

Darya was brutal to the women who served her. She was known for beating pregnant female serfs and pouring boiling water over others. Sometimes she would even break her serfs' bones before throwing them outside, naked, with no way back into their homes. While Darya wasn't known for killing men, she would punish them by ferociously murdering the women they loved. Later on, investigators would find that Darya was responsible for killing an estimated thirty-eight people over the span of six to seven years; three of her victims were men and some were girls as young as ten years old.

The deaths at the Saltykova estate were no secret; there were complaints, but many believe they were ignored by authorities because of the family's status in society. It wasn't until a handful of her victims' family members were able to convince the ruling empress, Catherine the Great, to take their petition seriously that Darya was arrested for her crimes. In the summer of 1762, two serfs—Sakhvely Martynov and Ermolay Ilyin—brought the petition to the empress, as Ermolay had personally seen three of his wives die at Darya's hand. Fortunately, Catherine decided to investigate the petition and Darya's alleged crimes because doing so aligned well with her personal goals: She had introduced a lawfulness initiative in 1762 in an attempt to cut down on crime.

Darya was jailed for six years while the investigation was underway, but she was released when none of her surviving victims would speak out against her when asked, leaving the police with no reason to keep her behind bars. It was the relatives of her dead victims who took the matter into their own hands, creating a petition for her punishment to present to Catherine the Great. On October 2, 1768, she was sentenced to her own lifetime of torture for the killings. Since the death penalty had been removed from Russian law in 1754, the empress had to get a little creative with Darya's punishment. In addition to being imprisoned in a windowless room in the basement of a convent, Darya was also given a "civil execution." This involved Darya being chained to a platform in the middle of Moscow's bustling Red Square so people could come and get a look at the ruthless serial killer. She was also forced to wear a sign that read "This woman has tortured and murdered."

After spending eleven years in the convent basement in complete darkness—the only light being a candle at mealtime—Darya was moved to a monastery building that had a single window with shutters. While imprisoned there, she became known for spitting at passersby and jabbing at them with sticks. At the age of seventy-one, thirty-three years after she was jailed, Darya died in her cell.

LAVINIA FISHER

The LEGENDARY HOTEL KILLER

———————⋙••⋘———————

I t's hard to separate fact from fiction when it comes to Lavinia Fisher, whom some people consider to be America's first female serial killer. According to historical records, she and her husband did *not* kill hundreds of people, as some tall tales have claimed. Only a handful of bodies were discovered on their inn's property and, according to the same records, Lavinia was never charged with murder. What has been confirmed was still a reason for death by hanging at the time, though: highway robbery. But before we get to Lavinia's doomed fate, let's start at the beginning of her and her husband's legendary story.

Lavinia and her husband, John Fisher, were owners and operators of the Six Mile Wayfarer House, an inn located six miles from downtown Charleston, South Carolina. As many inns were located near major cities in the early 1800s, they catered to travelers from all around the country, and many of these establishments had mile markers in their names, which made it easy for travelers to track where they were on their journey. Inns were much more than just a spot to sleep, though. Travelers could also expect to find a restaurant, a place for horses to eat and drink, and a gambling den on the premises if they were lucky.

John and Lavinia were well-liked in the community, but after they ran the inn for a while, rumors began to spread that patrons of the inn were going missing. The gossip mill churned until a group of people went to stake out the hotel in February 1819. As the story goes, they returned to town after a few hours without seeing any action, but did leave behind one person to keep an eye on the inn: David Ross.

The next day, David was supposedly kidnapped by a group of men and Lavinia. Throughout the attack, he looked to Lavinia for help; in response, she bashed him in the head. Somehow, though, he escaped the scene and reported the incident to local authorities. This was the first lead police had on the Fishers, according to legend. The second tip came when a traveler named John Peeples stopped at the inn on his way to Charleston from Georgia. Upon meeting Lavinia and inquiring about a room, he was told there were none available. As consolation, she invited him in for tea and dinner, which he accepted, and began asking him questions about his life while her husband looked on, quieter than his wife. Lucky for Peeples, he didn't like the tea she was serving, so in lieu of being impolite and not drinking it, he poured out his cup while Lavinia was distracted. She then told him that a room had suddenly become available. *How . . . convenient*, you're probably thinking.

After he settled into his room, Peeples started to feel uneasy about the personal information he had shared with Lavinia during their meal, so instead of sleeping in the bed, he opted to listen to his gut feeling of discomfort and fell asleep in a chair near the door. Luck, as I mentioned before, was on his side. In the middle of the night, he was awoken by a loud noise. The next detail is straight out of a psychological thriller, but again, please keep in mind that there is no official documentation that this actually happened: The bed *disappeared*.

According to what Peeples shared with authorities, the bed fell into a massive hole in the ground—one *he* was meant to fall into, had he been sleeping where Lavinia thought he would be. When it happened, he jumped out the window in response, quickly located his horse, and rushed into Charleston proper to alert the police.

As one version of the story goes, John and Lavinia were arrested on the spot and brought to jail to wait out their trial. There, they pleaded not guilty, but the jury did not rule in their favor. According to the same story, once in prison, John devised a plan for their escape, and even managed to pull part of it off by tying knots in his bedsheet and using it to climb out his jail cell window. On his way down, though, the sheet ripped, leaving Lavinia stuck inside. But like any good murderous husband, he turned himself back in to make sure Lavinia wouldn't be left all alone. How charming.

There is one similarity among the legends of Lavinia and John and what we can prove actually happened, though: They were convicted of a crime. Only it wasn't murder—it was officially marked as highway robbery, another pastime that eventually got them in trouble. In February 1820, the couple was executed for their acts. Some say John went quietly, praying before he was hanged, while Lavinia wore her wedding dress and screamed the entire way to the gallows. Again, we can't prove these to be facts, so consider this part of the legend.

The *Charleston Courier* ran an article on John and Lavinia on February 22, 1819, which noted: "In Saturday's *Courier*, we gave some particulars of the conduct of a set of outlaws, who have for a long time past infested the road in the vicinity of this city, and whose outrageous conduct had of late become insupportable." It then described an instance in which a group of outlaws, assumedly John and Lavinia included, attacked John Peeples. It makes no mention of the disappearing bed, poisoning, or excessive dinner conversation.

All legends and truth aside, Lavinia has become a popular topic for ghost stories (and ghost tours) in Charleston. Some people even swear you can still see her in the window of what was once the old jail building and in the Unitarian church graveyard.

MARIA "GOEIE MIE" SWANENBURG

The WOMAN WHO POISONED FUNERAL-GOERS

———◆>••<◆———

Chances are, you didn't know that Maria Swanenburg was, according to her kill count, one of the most prolific serial killers of her time. That's because there isn't a whole lot out there to remind us of her heinous crimes. Maria earned her nickname—"Goeie Mie" or "Good Mee"—for her reputation as a kind neighbor and friend who was always ready to help out someone in need. She was born in the Netherlands in 1839, but it wasn't until she was in her early forties that she started robbing and stealing from others. It's believed that she poisoned as many as ninety people between the years of 1864 and 1883.

Maria took advantage of the bleak atmosphere of Leiden, the city where she grew up: Sickness had spread through the region like a snowball gaining speed down a hill and people were dying all over the place. The area was avoided by doctors, in the interest of staying healthy themselves. With this working in her favor, Maria's victims and their causes of death were rarely questioned.

Maria's poison of choice was arsenic, which she often used to taint oatmeal or coffee. According to *Dutch News*, she was once responsible for poisoning multiple people attending a funeral by sneaking arsenic into their coffee at the service. Her motive was financial: During her trial, it came to light that she was taking out funeral insurance policies on her victims, and ultimately pulled in a good amount of money by cashing in.

It's hard to know exactly how many people Maria killed, but Stefan Glasbergen, author of *Goeie Mie: Biografie van een seriemoordenares*—often regarded as the sole resource on Maria's life—has traced twenty-three victims to the serial killer. Assuming this is true, Maria would be considered the most lethal female serial killer in history, followed by Jane Toppan, an American serial killer who was convicted of taking eleven lives (though she admitted to killing at least thirty-one).

Even more gruesome may be the fact that Maria also took the lives of her family members. Her father, Clemens Swanenburg, and her mother, Johanna Dingjan, were among the twenty-three people she murdered. Once this information became public, angry mobs attended her hearings and even attempted to harm her. It wasn't until May 1, 1885, that Marie was convicted of murder, at the age of forty-five. Her sentence was life imprisonment at a prison in Gorinchem, the Netherlands. She died in Gorinchem on April 11, 1915.

"JOLLY JANE" TOPPAN

The SADISTIC NURSE

F rom its beginning, Jane Toppan's story can only be described as grim. Jane, who was born Honora Kelley in 1854, grew up in a female asylum that was home to orphaned children in the Boston area. Her mother, Bridget, died of tuberculosis shortly after she gave birth, and Jane and her sister were relocated to the asylum after their father succumbed to alcoholism and was institutionalized. More often than not, children who were in this situation went on to have very difficult childhoods. Not much is known about Jane's sister, Delia, after she left the asylum—the only detail that's widely known is that she was forced into a life of sex work at a young age. Jane was put into foster care and raised by a widowed mother named Ann Toppan, who gave her the name Jane.

Jane ended up forming a strong relationship with Ann, and worked for years as indentured help around the Toppan home. When Jane turned eighteen, she was no longer required to perform her duties and was given a payment of $50 to start her life. Instead of leaving, however, she stayed on to continue helping the Toppan family. When Ann passed away and her biological daughter left home to marry, Jane moved on to the next phase of her life: nursing. After attending courses at Boston's Cambridge Hospital to gain her certification, she found work as a student nurse on the hospital campus. Maybe it was her experience tending to Ann and her family, but she found real purpose in getting to know the patients and keeping them under her care. However, at a certain point, things took a very dark turn.

In an attempt to keep her beloved patients close to her, Jane would forge paperwork and medical records that kept them in the hospital longer than they needed to be. These were just the smallest of her crimes, though. Finding herself drawn to her elderly patients, Jane became what many call an "angel of death," and she began experimenting on her patients with opium. To be specific, she would give them high doses of the drug, watch them react to it, and ultimately kill them. For the luckier victims, she would only administer enough to make them appear sickly so she could nurse them back to health. There's no official word on what caused her to begin this torture.

Jane's schooling at Cambridge Hospital had prepared her for a career as a private duty nurse, meaning she could care for people in their own homes, which was an even more ideal setting for abusing and poisoning her patients, and in 1891 she left the hospital campus to take on work for some of the most prominent families in the Boston area. When you consider the fact that Jane wasn't put on trial for her crimes until 1902, it's disturbing to think of the number of murders she was able to commit in those eleven years. In a statement to her attorney, Jane herself admitted to killing at least thirty-one during that period. Jane's victims also included a number of her own relatives, including her foster sister, Elizabeth.

"A true Jekyll-and-Hyde personality, she possessed a professional competence and affable charm that made her a valued companion to a large circle of people, who trusted her with their very lives," Harold Schechter writes in his book *Fatal: The Poisonous Life of a Female Serial Killer.* "Beneath her jovial exterior, however, there lurked a being of genuinely monstrous drives and appetites—an implacable sadist who derived intense, sexual pleasure from watching a succession of innocent victims perish slowly at her hands."[1] And there you have it, folks: the mic drop. It's not often you find a woman at the root of sadistic lust killing, and that's exactly what Schechter finds Jane's actions to be. This mask of sanity allowed Jane to become close to her victims before ultimately killing them. While there is no proof of the extent or presence of Jane's sexual activity with her victims, she did tell her attorney that she would occasionally share a bed with her patients as they were dying from her poison.

The murder that brought Jane's ghastly hobby to light was that of Minnie Gibbs, the daughter of Alden Davis (Jane's landlord). Minnie was actually Jane's last kill in the Gibbs family. She had made her way, quickly, through the three other members of the family first: Alden, Genevieve (Alden's sister), and Mattie (Alden's wife). Mattie was Jane's first kill of the family, on an unlucky day when she had come to collect overdue rent in Alden's place. Next was Alden; Jane moved in after Mattie's murder to take care of him. Genevieve and Minnie followed. After more than a decade of invisible murders, Jane's downfall was the result of a heartbroken man's gut suspicion. Minnie's father-in-law, Captain Paul Gibbs, was shocked that the family had all died so suddenly after seeming to be healthy. They had, for the most part, been perfectly fine the last time he had seen them and hadn't been suffering from any kind of illness or injury. Despite the seeming lack of suspicion for foul play, Captain Gibbs noticed a commonality among the deaths: Jane. She had cared for each member of the family at some point. When Captain Gibbs started suspecting Jane of murder, he began assembling his own team of investigators, starting with Leonard Wood, a military hero and close family friend with influential connections. Leonard then enlisted the help of a renowned toxicologist by the name of Dr. Edward S. Wood (no relation). Next came the involvement of Josephus Whitney, a state detective who ordered that the bodies of Genevieve and Minnie be exhumed for examination.

Jane was arrested on October 26, 1901, while she was visiting her friend Sarah Nichols in Amherst, New Hampshire. In the time since she had killed Minnie, Jane had returned to her hometown of Lowell, Massachusetts, to woo a man named Oramel Brigham, but in typical Jane Toppan fashion, she ultimately murdered his seventy-year-old sister, who lived with him, by giving her a lethal dose of morphine. The death of his sister spurred Oramel to kick Jane out of his home, which led to her eventual capture.

The *Boston Globe* described Jane's walk into the courthouse for her first trial, on October 31, 1901:

> *Miss Toppan was very pale, and beneath her jet black*
> *hair, but slightly streaked with gray, her sunken*
> *cheeks seemed very white, and there was the darkness*

beneath the eyes that showed that the night had not been a restful one in the county jail. She wore a black tailored skirt and jacket and a white shirtwaist with a band of black about her throat. Upon her head her hastily combed hair was concealed by a black hat trimmed with black muslin. She carried her gloves and veil, but even these light objects were a burden as she dropped them while ascending the two steps to the courthouse.[2]

It wasn't until June 1902 that Jane's fate was decided. After just twenty-seven minutes of deliberation, the jury, swayed by her insanity plea, pronounced her not guilty, and she was sentenced to life in Taunton State Hospital. Jane had a few thoughts to share on the jury's decision: "If I had been a married woman, I probably would not have killed all of those people," she said. "I would have had my husband, my children, and my home to take up my mind."[3]

She died in August 1938. Her obituary in the *Lowell Sun* highlighted her very public trial, of course, but also shined a bit of light on her personality: "In her school work, as in her profession in later years, she was one of the leaders of her class—brilliant and aggressive in all things."

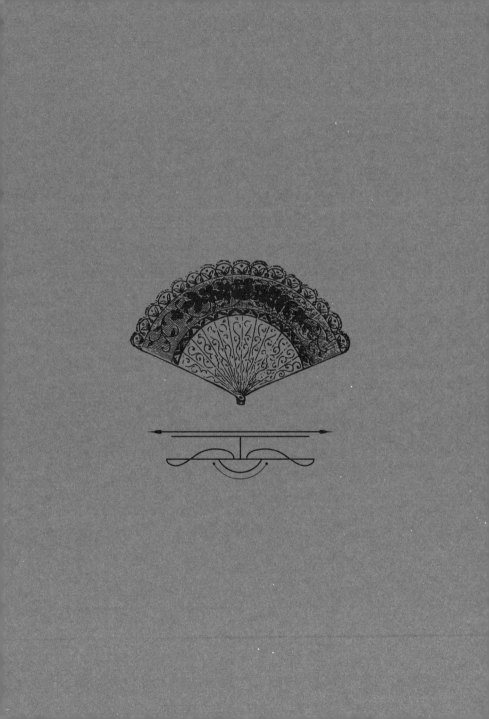

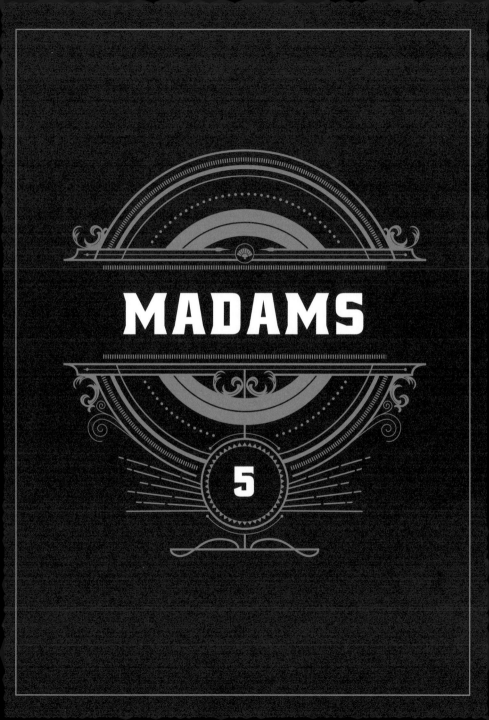

MADAMS

5

MORE THAN JUST
"LADIES OF THE NIGHT"

While today, the legitimacy of a job in sex work is hotly debated across the world, it was a booming illicit business throughout the United States during the Civil War. That being said, many "madams"—the title given to a woman who owned a brothel—still had to pay inflated taxes at times, depending on the location of their business. In other cases, the women working at the brothels also had to abide by special rules that set them apart from other people in society (think: special "shopping hours" that gave them the chance to visit certain stores only when ladies of more reputable social standing were not present). Some sex workers even had to pay fees in order to work in the brothels. The rules very much depended on the local government and the communities in which the brothels were located and whether they thought it benefitted or posed a threat to the local economy.

Brothels first gained popularity in the United States in the 1700s, and were typically located in cities with bustling ports. These early establishments provided recreation for men traveling alone in the US, as sex work at the time was generally viewed as a socially acceptable business. As brothels grew in number and started showing up in cities *without* ports, however, they began to cater to different audiences.

There were brothels that offered inexpensive services and others that provided a more luxe experience. And when sex work became more prevalent, society's opinion of the women who ran and worked in these establishments also changed. Although brothels and sex work were still legal in the 1700s, at a certain point, bribes and other financial agreements between madams and the local authorities became common in order to keep the peace. This meant that financial stakeholders, sex workers, and brothel owners would occasionally receive a fine or punishment of sorts. That being said, the actions against them were never particularly harsh or taken seriously.

In the late seventeenth and early eighteenth centuries, the first organized actions against brothels across the country occurred, a catastrophic series of events generally known as the Whorehouse Riots. At this time, local governments against the existence of brothels and sex work in their respective cities would encourage citizens to destroy the establishments by setting fire to them and tearing down whatever they could. As a result of these riots, in 1790 Massachusetts became the first state to make running a brothel illegal . . . but the law wouldn't stick.

For a century afterward, brothels existed as complicated parts of their local communities in the US. Some madams learned how to keep their houses afloat by keeping their reputations in balance, contributing to society in other important ways, such as through regular charity work. Others became adept at dodging ambushes set up by local authorities. And then there were those who offered such elevated experiences that only the wealthiest men could afford their prices, making it less of a financial burden to keep the brothel in business. In 1913, the federal government finally decided to leave the legality of brothels up to the states to decide. Currently, Nevada is the only state in which brothels are legal, and they're only legal within certain counties.

In this section, you will meet a group of women from the United States and beyond who not only broke the law but also didn't abide by other societal conventions imposed upon women during the time, whether by running their own businesses or in other ways.

One thing I will ask you to note: Throughout this chapter, I took care to refer to the people involved in this line of work as "sex workers," but "prostitutes" was an accepted term of the time.

Terms to Know

Brothel: An establishment where people can visit sex workers and pay for their services; these houses vary in level of luxury.

Bordello: Another term for brothel.

Keeping company: A euphemism used for when a sex worker is in session with a client; also refers to sex workers who have repeat clients.

Look-see: A brief look or inspection; also refers to sex workers who allow people to visit them for brief viewing periods for a set amount of money.

ELIZABETH CRESSWELL

The MADAM WHO LIVED "WELL"

—◆>••<◆—

A s with many women in this book, there isn't much information on record about Elizabeth Cresswell's early life. We do
know that she was a highly successful madam in London during the 1650s and ran more than one bordello offering options for
all budgets. King Charles II supposedly visited some of her "boarding homes" (this is unconfirmed, but speaks to her popularity), and
she was often targeted for her own political beliefs. Elizabeth was
a staunch Protestant and was not quiet about her opinions of the
monarchy, according to Don Jordan in his book *The King's City: A
History of London During the Restoration.* "Possessing a strongly
Protestant perspective on monarchy, she publicly and financially
supported the Whig point of view," he writes. "For her time, Cresswell was unusual—she was a woman who became financially independent through her own endeavors, albeit from running a string
of brothels, and publicly took part in the most important political
debate of her time."[1]

Early on in her career, Elizabeth was a sex worker. She gained
popularity and eventually opened up her own boarding house in
Bartholomew Close, a location just a couple of hundred yards away
from Saint Paul's Cathedral in London. She was one of many who
were making money from being a madam during this time period
in London, but hiring high-class women—some reportedly of noble
standing—is what set her apart from the competition. She quickly
opened a number of brothels, each one catering to all budgets and
tastes. Elizabeth and her agents would search the countryside for

new girls to hire, often finding beautiful women who had experienced hard times and were searching for a new beginning. Introducing new sex workers to her lineup and a steady advertising plan kept her front-of-mind with her clients. Today, I have no doubt Elizabeth would have taken well to the role of social media influencer, given her knack for self-promotion centuries before it became a cultural phenomenon. She became a favorite for all her efforts in running her business. For this reason, she was often the subject of plays, satires, and other propaganda in London.

But it was her political opinions that led to her eventual downfall. Her brothels were attacked in the Bawdy House Riots of 1688, a series of days during which government apprentices ran about London, ransacking and setting fire to the most popular bordellos. In response, Elizabeth sponsored a satirical pamphlet titled "The Poor-Whores' Petition," which was delivered directly to Lady Castlemaine (aka Barbara Villiers), the king's mistress. The royal court of the time was known to be stacked with clientele for these brothels, who helped look out for the safety of the establishments and, many times, assisted them in avoiding consequences in gray-area legal situations. The pamphlet was a satirical plea for help, likening Lady Castlemaine to a sister of the women affected by the riots and asking for her empathy and support in their time of need. I bet you can guess her response to the letter: fury at being compared to the city's sex workers.

The rage against the pamphlet deeply affected Elizabeth, who, as its sponsor, was suddenly on everyone's minds. Her previous debts were called in, and the women working for her were asked to speak out against their employer. The latter is what got Elizabeth in real trouble—her girls did speak of her tough character as a boss, and she was sentenced and sent to Bridewell Prison. Elizabeth spent her last years there, dying in the prison sometime around 1698, according to various historical records. Her last wish was for a preacher to conduct her funeral service and only speak highly of her. She offered ten British pounds for the task, and someone was found to carry out her wishes. Here is what was said about Elizabeth's life, according to Catharine Arnold's book *City of Sin: London and Its Vices*:

> *By the Will of the Deceased it is expected that I should mention and say nothing but Well of her. All that I shall say of her therefore is this. She was born well, she liv'd well and she died well, for she was born with the name Cresswell, she lived in Clerkenwell and she died in Bridewell.*[2]

Well played.

AH TOY

The ENTREPRENEURIAL MADAM

Transport yourself to San Francisco, 1848. Chinatown hadn't yet been officially established. There was a gold rush in the north. Ah Toy, a striking twenty-year-old woman with an infectious personality, has just arrived in the city, and is one of the first Chinese women to settle in California.[1] She had been brought across the Pacific Ocean as an enslaved person, but the tides turned for Ah Toy when the person who "owned" her died en route to America. Suddenly, Ah Toy was in San Francisco on her own, free to better her living situation, and she did precisely that, though many might not have chosen the same path.

In China, Ah Toy was seen as "too tall, too broad-shouldered," with feet that were "too big." In the US, however, none of those things seemed to matter as much. Ah Toy had a new lease on life. Soon after arriving in San Francisco, she met a police officer by the name of John A. Clark, who began "keeping company" with her, or visiting as a client. In the mid-1800s, people weren't used to seeing someone of Chinese descent in California, and Ah Toy used this to gain an advantage over competitors. She always had a line of men waiting to visit with her at her modest home on Clay Street. Ah Toy was attracting those who wanted to see the "physiological differences between Western and Asian females" according to a January 1998 article published in the *San Francisco Chronicle*.[2] It was said that the lines leading up to her door were longest on days when ships docked in the nearby harbor. In 1850, two short years after she had arrived in San Francisco, Ah Toy opened up her own "boarding home" and hired five Chinese women to work for her. The bordello was located on Pike Street Alley, a street that has since been renamed Waverly Place and which you can still visit today.

As more women traveled to California from China in the hopes of finding work and a better way of life, Ah Toy would be the first to survey the newcomers and offer those she considered the most beautiful a job at her bordello. As one of the first women from her home country to settle in San Francisco, she gained quite a reputation in the area, and her clients—as well as other brothel owners—regarded her with the utmost respect. However, many women did not experience the warm welcome Ah Toy did: Often, women in a similar situation were harassed by the locals upon setting foot on land, and stripped naked for inspection. According to *Cowgirl* magazine, many of these women were even sold to brothel owners or men on the hunt for a mistress, for prices between $30 and $90 in China and between $300 and $3,000 in California.[3]

Ah Toy was known for far more than being beautiful and entrepreneurial, though. She also played an important role in fighting the racism that pervaded the local courts at the time. Her first introduction to the United States legal system came after she caught a handful of her clients trying to pay with counterfeit brass coins. Ah Toy brought the criminals to court, but the charges were dismissed. This was only the beginning of her unlucky encounters with the law. To know the extent of the unfairness she endured, keep in mind that brothel owners during the mid-1800s were often left alone as long as they cooperated with the authorities and lawmakers, which led many people to believe her run-ins with the law were due to her race. Ah Toy was arrested in 1854 and subsequently convicted for "keeping a disorderly house," which, again, was unusual for madams of the time. For three years, she dealt with these legal quandaries and further arrests. In 1857, she decided she couldn't deal with them anymore and sold her brothel.

Ah Toy took her money—which amounted to quite a fortune at the time—and everything she owned and moved back to China to live out her days . . . then she had a change of heart. In March 1959, she returned to California and once again stepped into the role of madam. But a few short weeks later, she was hit with yet another charge for keeping a disorderly house—and it seems the pressure did a number on her. Five months after returning to San Francisco, she was accused of, arrested for, and fined for beating one of the women she employed. In September of the same year, she was arrested and charged with running a brothel. At this point, with at least four convictions under her belt, Ah Toy disappeared.

As with most legends, people have their own ideas of where Ah Toy went. Most believe she returned to China. But no matter where Ah Toy ended up, you can't help but applaud the woman for trying to pave her own path in a foreign and often hostile city.

KATE ELDER

DOC HOLLIDAY'S GAL

———◆>••<◆———

Kate Elder, born Mary Katharine Haroney (sometimes spelled Horoney), had a childhood that must have felt a bit like living inside a pinball machine. She was born in Hungary on November 7, 1850, and received the best education possible, thanks to her father's wealth and standing in society. She also reportedly spoke a number of languages, including Hungarian, Spanish, English, and French. When her father, a physician, was assigned to be the personal surgeon to Mexico's Emperor Maximilian I in 1862, the Haroney family made the move from Hungary to Mexico. Despite Kate's education, moving from the comfortable and familiar atmosphere in which she had grown up and taking a step closer to the world of the Wild West could not have been an easy transition.

For three years, Kate and her family lived in Mexico, until Emperor Maximilian's government fell in 1865, when Kate was fourteen years old, sending the Haroney family fleeing to—I'll give you a beat to try to guess what's coming next—Davenport, Iowa. This is where things began to crumble. Shortly after the move, Kate's mother fell ill and died from an unknown cause. Kate's father, the surgeon, followed her in death about a year later. This left Kate orphaned, and she was eventually placed in foster care with a man named Otto Smith.

Her adventurous life began when Kate, at seventeen, left Otto and hitched a ride on a steamboat headed toward St. Louis, Missouri. Luckily, the boat's captain was an empathetic man by the name of Captain Fisher. He pitied her situation and took her under his wing once they docked. She took his name and became Kate Fisher before enrolling in a convent school in St. Louis. But don't let this seemingly innocent education lead you astray—Kate would soon enter a dark world rife with murder, sex work, and more seedy characters than you can count.

The years between her graduation from the convent school and her arrival in Dodge City, Kansas, in 1874 are a blur; there isn't much historical documentation on where she was or what she was doing. Some claim she married a dentist named Silas Melvin and had a child, but there is no record of the marriage or any birth; Kate claimed both her husband and her child died, so this information is pretty dubious. In any case, we meet up with Kate again in Dodge City, 1874, where she was now hiding behind the name Kate Elder.

Kate found a job as a sex worker at a brothel owned by Nellie "Bessie" Earp. If that last name rings a bell, there's a good reason for it. Bessie was married to James Earp, who was the older brother of Virgil Earp, a known Wild West character who was friendly with Doc Holliday. Kate worked at the brothel for four years and formed a friendship with Bessie and her family that, in 1877, took her to Fort Griffin, Texas. Kate was still employed as a sex worker in Texas, but she found herself much more involved with the comings and goings of the local outlaws, as well as Wyatt Earp—a deputy marshal in Tombstone, Arizona, and another of James's brothers—and Doc, who were close friends. There is one tale in particular that put her in the admirable sights of Doc and kicked off their romantic relationship.

Wyatt would tell anyone who would listen about the time Doc slashed his opponent's belly open during a game of poker. After he looked at one too many cards from the discard pile—after being warned not to, as it was a very strict violation of the game—Doc pulled in the game pot for himself. This action caused his opponent, a well-known local bully, to pull out his pistol. Acting in self-defense, Doc pulled out his knife and killed his adversary. He didn't flee the scene, as he felt confident in his plea of self-defense, but was still arrested for the killing. He was put in a local hotel room, since there wasn't a jail in Fort Griffin at the time. Upon hearing the news, Kate, armed with two pistols, set fire to a shed near the hotel where Doc was being held, busied everyone with putting it out, and found the police officer tasked with keeping Doc in the room. She disarmed the officer and helped Doc escape. They made their way back to Dodge City under the cover of night on stolen horses. Romantic, right?

From Dodge City, they hit the road, visiting Las Vegas and Deadwood. After renting a boarding house for a short period in Globe, Arizona, Kate wound up running her own bordello in Tombstone. Doc joined her there after spending time in Tucson feeding his faro and poker hobby, and the couple jumped right back into their relationship.

For nearly five years, they were able to make their partnership last, despite it being notoriously turbulent and volatile. It wasn't until Kate made a drunken mistake that they had a real falling out. In 1881, the authorities caught word of a highway robbery they believed Doc had been involved with. While he *wasn't* one of the people involved in the act, he was close friends with people who *were*. Knowing that Doc and Kate had just finished up a big fight, Doc's enemies went to Kate, got her drunk, and convinced her to tell the police that Doc had been part of the robbery. On her word, Doc was arrested. His jail time was short-lived, as Kate redacted her statement the next morning, but their relationship was forever damaged.

Doc and Kate split ways, with her heading back to Globe and Doc to Glenwood Springs, Colorado, but they would meet one last time at Doc's home to say their goodbyes in 1887, right before he died. After Doc passed, Kate met another man in Colorado, George Cummings, a blacksmith. The pair was together for a year before separating. Kate then found work in Cochise, Arizona, for a short while before heading to Dos Cabezas, Arizona, to become a housekeeper for a man named John Howard. She remained employed by Howard until his death in 1930.

Kate spent her final years living at the Arizona Pioneers' Home under the name Kate Cummings. The home was a state-run housing project for aging Arizona residents who had helped settle the area. She died at that home on November 2, 1940, a few days short of her ninetieth birthday. But this wasn't before she was able to share the story fans of the Wild West and Doc Holliday had been waiting for: what really happened in the moments immediately following the infamous Gunfight at the O.K. Corral on Wednesday, October 26, 1881. When she was eighty-nine, she wrote a letter detailing Doc's reaction after the shots were fired.

For the uninformed, here's a breakdown of the short-lived fight: A disagreement during a round of gambling the night before had a man named Ike Clanton searching for Doc, rifle in hand, at C. S. Fly's boarding house, where Doc was staying. He was turned away at the door, but word that he had made an appearance only added fuel to the fire that eventually manifested as a true Wild West shootout at the O.K. Corral. Doc and the Earp brothers gathered and set up a lookout for the rest of Clanton's crew, who eventually showed up in a vacant lot near the corral. In a matter of thirty seconds, at least thirty gunshots were fired, killing three and injuring Doc Holliday. Kate was able to provide some important context on Doc's state of mind after the fight, sharing that he returned to his room at Fly's and said, "That was awful, just awful," while breaking down into sobs.

PEARL DE VERE

The MADAM WHO DIED
at HER OWN PARTY

———◆>••<◆———

We're going to start Pearl de Vere's story in Cripple Creek, Colorado, in 1893. The small town was booming thanks to an increase in miners searching for gold in the surrounding mountains. Pearl's introduction to sex work happened before she landed in Cripple Creek. Previously, she resided in Denver and amassed a solid savings from her work in a bordello that provided services for the city's wealthiest men. Not much is known about Pearl's life before she lived in Denver. Some believe that she made dresses for the wealthy women of Evansville, Indiana, where it's thought she grew up. But in Cripple Creek, she was ready to take her career to the next level and opened up her own brothel in a small home on Myers Avenue. Pearl's bordello was the definition of an overnight success, a desirable place of recreation for the tired miners overtaking the town.

Pearl was thirty-one when she opened up her brothel. She was a striking woman with dyed red hair, pale skin, and a notably strong will and business vision. Just as much as she valued her own beauty, Pearl expected her employees to keep up their appearances in the same way. They were regularly tested for STDs, received fair compensation, and wore beautiful clothes. Pearl herself would parade throughout the mining camp in a horse-led carriage wearing the latest fashions, capturing the attention of every man and woman on the site.

As it often goes in small towns, people began to talk. The women of Cripple Creek weren't especially enthused by Pearl's girls shopping

alongside them. They raised enough of a fuss that the local authority, Marshal Wilson, set up separate "shopping hours" for "working
girls," which often fell during the stores' off hours. These women
were also required to pay a new tax of $6 a month to keep their jobs.
Madams got it worse, owing $16 a month for running their establish-
ments. All extra costs aside, Pearl and her girls thrived and gained
popularity. Because of this, Pearl became a somewhat notorious figure in the community, especially in the eyes of local women and children, the latter of which were told never to visit or even *make eye
contact on* Myers Street.

Pearl eventually met a mill owner by the name of C. B. Flynn, and
they married in 1895. She continued to run her business in Cripple
Creek, but tragedy struck shortly after their marriage, when a fire
stormed through the mining camp, destroying both Pearl's bordello
and C. B.'s mill. While many of the town's businesses were ruined, as
well as the will of many business owners, Pearl and C. B. persevered.
She remained in Cripple Creek to rebuild her brothel while C. B. left
for Monterrey, Mexico, to take a job smelting steel and iron. Pearl's
hard work rebuilding her business was well received: In 1896, she
opened the most beautiful brothel the town had ever seen.

Pearl named her new endeavor the Old Homestead and made it
impossible for anyone other than the wealthiest gentlemen to pay a
visit. First off, to even gain entry, you needed references. From there,
a night at the brothel would run $250. To give you an idea of how much
money that was at the time, consider that a miner made, on the high
end, $3 a day. Pearl's place was filled with rich visitors looking to take
in the best Cripple Creek had to offer. Four women worked in Pearl's
brothel, and when they were on the job, they were surrounded by the
most expensive furnishings: wallpaper from Paris, luxurious carpets,
leather gaming tables, hardwood furniture, and—the best part of all—
two bathrooms. Needless to say, reservations were necessary.

The Old Homestead was a popular spot for larger-than-life parties, the most famous of which happened on June 4, 1897. Dressed in a pink chiffon dress that reportedly cost $800 at the time, Pearl hosted a soiree for a millionaire from Poverty Gulch, Colorado, who had taken a liking to her. Aside from inviting the wealthiest and most prominent people from local society, Pearl brought in caviar from Russia, champagne from France, and Wild Turkey liquor from Kentucky, too. Guests were also treated to performances by two orchestras hailing from Denver. The night would have gone perfectly, had it not been for one deadly mistake Pearl made on her way to bed.

After drinking a touch too much, she excused herself and headed to her bedroom to call it a night. At the time, ingesting a bit of morphine to aid sleep was not unheard of—Pearl just took too much that night. One of her girls checked on her in the middle of the night and, noticing that Pearl was still in her party dress and having trouble breathing, she called for a doctor. But it was too late. Later, it was determined that Pearl had unintentionally overdosed on morphine. Her body was sent to Fairley Bros. & Lampman Undertakers, who alerted her surviving family.

Pearl's sister made the trek from Indiana to Cripple Creek, where she learned of her sister's true career. She had been under the impression that Pearl had been making dresses this entire time, not entertaining men at her own brothel. Needless to say, Pearl's dyed-red hair was the least shocking part of it all. Her sister left without assuming any responsibility for Pearl's body.

However, there was another surprise in store. With no one to handle the cost of burying Pearl, the undertakers looked to her estate, but quickly found out that looks can be deceiving: Pearl did not have enough money to her name for a proper burial. The idea was floated to sell the pink chiffon dress she died in for funds, but was quickly turned down, as someone from Denver—likely a past client or an admirer—wired the $1,000 necessary for a burial before any other action could be taken.

As you can imagine, the funeral was widely attended. Her funeral parade was led by a band and required four police escorts. Her casket—lavender in color—was covered in roses. The Old Homestead lived on without Pearl, welcoming gentlemen until 1917. From then on, it served as a boarding house (not to be confused with a *brothel* boarding house) and later was converted to a private home. In June 1958, the home was turned into a museum; the owners appreciated many of the items that were original to Pearl's brothel and wanted to give them a place to be displayed. Today, you can still see some of the Old Homestead's original furniture and take tours of the parlor, a wonderfully preserved exhibit of brothel history.

ADA AND MINNA EVERLEIGH

The MADAM SISTERS *with a* PENCHANT *for* OPULENCE

isters Minna and Ada Everleigh created their last name—I'll call it a stage name of sorts—based on their grandmother's letter sign-off: "Everly Yours." The duo, born in the US south, did pretty much everything together. They escaped bad marriages together and traveled together across the country as actresses. Minna and Ada eventually settled down in Chicago, but not before they kicked off their career by owning a brothel in Omaha, Nebraska, in the early 1900s. Surprisingly, though, that's not the bordello that made them famous.

In 1900, they took up residence inside a set of brownstones at

2131-33 S. Dearborn Street in Chicago. According to an article in the *Chicago Tribune*, the brothel they ran from this address boasted more than fifty rooms—a true mansion—each with its own theme. There was one called the Gold Room, which was filled with gold furnishings that gleamed under the lights, and another deemed the Chinese Room, where visitors were invited to set off firecrackers indoors. Simply entering Minna and Ada's brothel was a party in itself. Their business was built around providing sensual pleasure for their clients and attracted a wide crowd of married men looking for adventurous partners. The women who worked at their club were even referred to as "butterflies."

Before opening their brothel, the sisters had traveled around the country and met with madams to gather a list of tips for running their own business. The clientele the sisters were after had money—and lots of it—and they found their audience in abundance in Chicago, a city experiencing a swift increase in population and commercial growth. A visit to their house was a full night's experience, starting with drinks and dinner (without any women), followed by whatever relationship a visitor wanted to pay for that night. A bottle of champagne cost $12. Dinner at the brothel started at $50. (That's almost $350 and $1,500 today, respectively.) Anyone who wasn't up for the dinner price was advised to steer clear of the sisters' opulent business—but many didn't bat an eye at the cost.

This was enough excitement for Ada and Minna. While they managed to avoid a jail sentence for operating a brothel, the law eventually interfered with their gold mine. The sisters had created a leather-bound brochure showcasing photos of the club's interior, accompanied by words written by Ada herself. This book fell into the hands of Chicago mayor Carter Harrison Jr., who decided to shut down the Everleigh Club in an effort to clean up the city's commercial districts. He did allow the women to throw one last party before the doors to the brothel were officially closed on October 11, 1911.

After their final rager, the sisters shut down their business, took on new names, and moved to New York City to live quiet lives. They blended into the background, and reportedly started a poetry circle. At the end of it all, they had raked in more than a million dollars in earnings—quite a take-home salary for the early 1900s. They stuck together until Minna died in 1948, after which Ada left for Virginia with the money she made from selling the remainder of their belongings from the Chicago brothel. She lived in Virginia until she died in 1960, at the age of ninety-three.

FANNIE PORTER

The CHARMING BUSINESSWOMAN FAVORED by the WILD BUNCH

Fannie Porter was the woman behind a brothel loved by outlaws on their journeys to and from San Antonio, Texas. Her boarding house was known to offer some of the most luxurious amenities of the time, including silk linens, lush carpets, fine glassware, and—if you were one of her favorite visitors—chilled champagne. The building itself was a two-story structure erected in 1883 and intended to be run as a boarding home . . . and Fannie continued to call it a "boarding home" for years to come, despite pivoting from her original business model. The property wasn't far from San Antonio's red-light district—in fact, it was about a block away, located in the city's second ward on the corner of Durango and San Saba Streets.

In 1893, San Antonio had local laws that protected establishments such as Fannie's, as long as the owners cooperated with the authorities and city officials. She only fell victim to one arrest in her career as a madam: She was brought in for vagrancy, a common charge related to prostitution in the late 1800s. Considering some of her best customers were famed outlaws, this point is especially intriguing. Fannie knew how to keep quiet and protect the reputations of her favored clients, and that was as good as gold for criminals on the run who were looking for a place to rest (and then some) for the night. Additionally, Fannie was known far and wide for her employees. The women she hired to work in her boarding house—there were five, according to the 1900 census—were different from others in the industry: They were expected to keep up their hygiene and remain free of STDs, making this particular brothel one of the more popular spots in the area. In fact, her establishment is purported to be the place where Harry Alonzo Longabaugh, better known as the Sundance Kid, met his partner, Etta Place.

But let's paint a picture of the woman who ran this tight ship: Fannie was a tough lady, according to historical records. She was known for giving the police a tough time when they visited her bordello, often chasing them off the property with a broom. Fannie herself was stunning, her eye-catching good looks partly due to her confidence as a successful entrepreneur. She always wore her brown hair stylishly piled on top of her head and dresses that showed off her tiny waist. Her charm put visitors at ease.

One of Fannie's most appreciated characteristics was her discretion; whenever someone paid a visit to her bordello, they didn't have to worry about showing up on the front page of the local paper or becoming the subject of town gossip. Many madams at the time were prone to sharing the names of their customers with the authorities and other interested parties, for the right price, but Fannie knew how to keep a secret. One thing that did make the news, though, was her going-away party for Butch Cassidy and his infamous Wild Bunch gang in February 1901. The authorities were catching on to the gang's crimes, which forced the outlaws to begin planning their disbandment. Before they went their separate ways, Fannie threw them a party to wish them well on their future endeavors.

After her most loyal customers split up and left the area, Fannie continued to run her "boarding house" for a number of years. Eventually, our leading lady faded into the background of history, and there are no historical records that confirm exactly what happened to her. Some claim a car crash in El Paso took her life sometime in 1940, and others think she lived out her days a wealthy woman alongside a husband she met after her career as a madam. The location of the boarding house at 503 Urban Loop in San Antonio lived many lives after Fannie left, most notably as a Boys & Girls Club in the mid-1990s. Today, the area is mainly used as parking for guests staying at the neighboring Holiday Inn Hotel.

TILLY DEVINE

The AUSSIE MADAM

T illy Devine could attribute her success as a madam to a loophole in an Australian law that claimed, in the 1920s, no *man* could own a brothel. Being a woman, Tilly determined that she was both an exception to the rule and fit for the business, so she gave it a try. In collaboration with her husband, Jim Devine, and Kate Leigh, an all-around criminal also living in Sydney, Australia, at the time, she opened up her own brothel. Jim told her stories of wealth, promising Tilly a gilded future. But Jim's entire career quickly began to revolve around Tilly's sex work: He even became her professional car-for-hire, which also made him Tilly's getaway driver. Despite having a partner in crime, Tilly racked up seventy-nine prostitution-related charges (think: indecent language and offensive behavior) between June 1921 and May 1925.

Given her many court appearances, she became a fixture in the public eye, drawing a crowd whenever she appeared for a trial. In May 1925, she pushed the limits of her arrests, and was convicted for slashing a man with a razor in a barbershop. She served two years in jail for the crime.

Jim and Tilly's relationship was far from ideal. His promises of wealth, which included a share of his family's kangaroo farm, proved to be lies. Perhaps living with such an unlikely and—to a big extent—unwanted partner contributed to Tilly's rough-and-tough attitude. She would demand to enter bars and be treated as an equal at a time in history when women were often not welcomed in such places. She was known for causing physical harm—like setting crooked cops on *fire*—when someone gave her any trouble. To put it bluntly, she wouldn't take any—and I mean *any*— bullshit.

It's no surprise, then, that the years after Tilly's release from jail were tumultuous. They resulted in more arrests and a "voluntary" one-year leave back in her home country of England. But by September 1939, Tilly had managed to get her act together and was running a handful of brothels across Sydney. She hired security and bouncers to help protect her girls, as well as the many visiting soldiers who would stop by on their comings and goings to and from the city. Instead of being known for her rash acts of violence or many court appearances, Tilly became better recognized for her lavish parties and the jewels she would wear during them. She also became a big financial supporter of the ongoing World War II. With her newfound independence and confidence, she had less room for Jim in her life.

It also didn't help that he was becoming more violent toward her. Tilly eventually sought a divorce on the grounds of cruelty.

She eventually remarried—this time to a seaman named Eric Parsons—and continued to run her business from the brothel she owned on Palmer Street, where she hosted clients until 1968. The final decades of her business became more and more expensive; taxes for recreational buildings were hefty and the fines continued to pile up.

Compared to her early, more adventurous life, Tilly's death was quiet. She died at the Concord Repatriation General Hospital in Sydney on November 24, 1970, after suffering from chronic bronchitis for two decades, but her legend lived on, inspiring tall tales and stories more grounded in reality, like the play *The Slaughter of St Teresa's Day*, which is based on Tilly's life.

PAULINE TABOR

The MADAM with TWO LIFESTYLES

——————

Pauline Tabor liked to keep her business pursuits and her family life separate—*very* separate. The madam was accustomed to running her brothels in states other than the one where she lived, in order to steer any negative talk or reputation damage away from her children.

Pauline was first introduced to sex work after hosting a party in November 1933 in her home, an unassuming white, Colonial-style house located on Smallhouse Road in Bowling Green, Kentucky.

Opening a business in the middle of the Great Depression was risky, but Pauline was recently divorced and ready to take control of her income in order to support her two sons and her mother. Prior to opening the brothel, she was selling makeup and hosiery door to door. In the house on Smallhouse Road, Pauline worked her way up in terms of clientele, eventually welcoming prominent politicians and military men to the establishment.

At a certain point, Pauline had saved enough money to buy a bigger brothel: a moderately sized building on Clay Street. Running a brothel was legal at the time, but Pauline experienced added difficulties, given Bowling Green's location in the Bible Belt. Rumors were prone to fly around the city, and Pauline was careful to protect her children from any gossip about her line of work. She kept quiet, depriving herself of any real social life outside her business. She also made sure the women she employed did not run around the city unsupervised, lest any unfortunate situations find them. She treated her employees well, bringing them to a medical center once a week for STD testing, paying them a solid wage, and giving them one week off every month to spend with their families. There was no alcohol allowed in the home, and Pauline made sure to turn away any drunk clients for the safety of her girls. She also didn't allow any nudity on the ground floor of the brothel. In short, her bordello was as upscale as they came.

Pauline herself looked nothing like her fellow madams. Many referred to her as Grandmother Pauline, a nod to her gray hair and matronly way of dressing. She was also constantly trying to better the lives of those around her. While she herself never saw clients, when asked how much she would charge had she chosen that life for herself, she reportedly told Bowling Green historian Mary Lucas, "I'd charge by the pound, and no one could afford me."[1]

One of the defining elements of Pauline's brothels was the milk can she set out in front of each one to mark that it was open for business. At a certain point, she had to attach metal chains to the cans, as they were often stolen from her properties. As popular as the bordello in Bowling Green was, the city became more cautious about the reputation these kinds of businesses had. There were many people who tried to take down Pauline's house, but she was smart about building up her protection. She regularly donated to children's foundations and political parties of all kinds in order to avoid bias. Local charities often looked to her to provide clothing, food, and coal to the less fortunate. However, trouble did eventually find its way into Pauline's home after a group of soldiers from Fort Knox (now known as Fort Campbell) visited her house.

There was an STD outbreak at the military base, and one of the soldiers who had visited Pauline's place reported her to the local police. At the time, there was a law restricting any brothel or related business activity within one hundred miles of a military base. Pauline was arrested, though her massive local popularity helped her get out of jail in just thirty minutes, after she was bailed out by an unknown supporter. But this incident sparked a long string of raids on Pauline's brothel, which were ordered by a disgruntled US legislator. Before each raid, she would get a warning from the local police force, as they recognized and appreciated what she contributed to the local community, and when the raid began, Pauline could be found in the front room, knitting with one of her employees.

The real culprit, if you could call it that, behind the downfall of Pauline's brothel business was city growth. Around 1968, a city development project took possession of most of the Clay Street area—including the brothel—demolished the existing buildings, and built low-income housing in their place. Pauline was then faced with the tricky decision of reopening her brothel or quitting the industry for good. She chose the latter.

After tying up all her loose ends in Bowling Green, Pauline moved to Plano, Texas, to be closer to her son. There, she bought a

120-acre organic farm, on which she led a very different life than the one she'd known in her role as a madam in Bowling Green society. In her memoir, *Pauline's: Memoirs of the Madam on Clay Street*, she wrote of her new life: "I'm much too busy enjoying my life, my children and grandchildren, my friends, a lovely country home, a healthy bank account, and priceless memories of a happy marriage."

Her two careers could not have been more different, but Pauline remained the same kind woman she always was, loved by neighbors for her frequent gifts of preserved vegetables, which she grew and canned herself. When she died in 1992, her body was returned to Bowling Green, where she was buried in a family plot.

Pauline's story in particular is one of my favorites in this collection: You truly can never judge a book by its cover.

OUTLAWS, GUNSLINGERS & BANDITS

6

WILD WOMEN

I f there's only one thing I want you to remember from this section, it's that women can be just as intimidating, terrifying, and feared as men. Even so, when you hear the word "outlaw," you're likely to think of a man first. Maybe it's Billy the Kid, Doc Holliday, Jesse James, or Butch Cassidy. But alongside these infamous men—sometimes even saving their lives—were a whole lot of women.

There were plenty of ladies who fell into the categories of "outlaw," "gunslinger," or "bandit." And, like those infamous men, their stories are often romanticized, exaggerated, and turned into legends. Many of the women in this chapter, like Rose Dunn and Etta Place, are hard to really *know*, given the mystery surrounding their upbringing and other facts as basic as their given names. Splitting the fact from the fiction is a near-impossible task, thanks to the many movies and books that have turned their lives into bedtime stories over the generations since they lived. It's just as important to know the fact from the fiction, as well as how the fiction was inspired by the fact.

Almost every story you hear about a female outlaw will have some sort of romantic affair tied to it. Many times, this *was* the case: Famous outlaws leading dangerous lives had tumultuous romances. Often, girlfriends and wives became accomplices. The outlaw community—specifically in the Wild West, which saw most of its action between 1850 and 1890—was also a small one. Many of the women profiled in the pages that follow knew each other or fled to the same hideaway houses. Ultimately, you may find reading about the women of the Wild West to be a fascinating look into a unique world of female relationships.

Terms to Know

Outlaw: A person who has broken the law; often someone who has not been caught and remains "at large."

Hideaway house: A place where outlaws would often go to avoid the authorities; these places were highly secure secret locales.

Stagecoach: A large horse-drawn vehicle; a popular method of travel during the Wild West era.

Gunslinger: A person who carried a gun and was known to shoot very well.

Banknote: A piece of paper money; acts as a central bank's promissory note to pay a stated sum to the bearer on demand.

Sharpshooter: Someone who is highly skilled at shooting a gun.

Bandit: A robber or outlaw, who often belongs to a specific gang; usually based in lawless and remote regions.

MARY FIELDS

"STAGECOACH MARY"

A s opposed to many of the other women in this book, Mary Fields was never arrested for breaking any written laws, but I've included her in this group of lawbreaking ladies for her boundary-breaking actions and subversive behavior. She was known for her intimidating temper, and got herself into plenty of trouble; some incidents may have landed her in jail or worse if she had been alive today. But although she may seem like an antagonistic person, she was actually a trailblazing woman who became a beloved member of her community.

Mary was born into slavery, and little is known about her early life; enslaved people were often referred to by a number as opposed to a name in record-keeping books of the time, making it hard to track down a particular person's birth date or place of birth. So her story starts after the Civil War, after Mary was emancipated. According to the *Encyclopaedia Britannica*, in the late 1870s, Mary became a housekeeper for the convent of the Ursuline Sisters in Toledo, Ohio, after working as a laundress and servant on riverboats traveling up the Mississippi River.

At the convent, Mary became close with the mother superior, Mother Amadeus Dunne. Some accounts believe Mother Amadeus was a member of the same family that had enslaved Mary, which may explain how Mary got to the convent, but there is no official confirmation that this was the case. One thing that would become clear in the future was that this friendship would be an important one for Mary, and would continue after Mother Amadeus left the convent to perform mission work in another state.

At the convent, Mary completed some of the more labor-focused tasks, which she took on with ease, given her natural strength (she stood six feet tall and weighed 200 pounds). But Mary's presence at the convent was not always well-received. There are historical records sharing the nuns' distaste for what they perceived to be her poor attitude, swearing, and unseemly temper. It might be fair to say that many of the sisters were relieved when, in 1885, Mary was called to join Mother Amadeus at St. Peter's Mission, a convent in Cascade, Montana, that focused on mission work, after Mother Amadeus fell gravely ill. Mary traveled to the convent and helped nurse Mother Amadeus back to health. But Mary's temper allegedly got in the way once again. During a verbal fight with a janitor at St. Peter's Mission, she pulled her gun. She was not arrested for the act, but the incident got Mary kicked out of the convent.

She gained her nickname, Stagecoach Mary, after receiving a job as the mail carrier for the US Postal Service, covering a route between St. Peter's Mission and the town of Cascade. This gig put her on the chart as the second woman and the very first African American woman to get a job as a contracted route mail carrier. Mary's job was a dangerous one, often filled with bandits and other shady characters looking for trouble and mail cars to rob. However, her stature, gun-toting confidence, and tendency to wear men's clothing helped her protect the stagecoach (donated by Mother Amadeus) carrying the convent's mail. She kept this job for eight years.

Though her boisterous nature and quick-fire temper gained her enemies throughout Cascade, her work as a mail carrier made her many friends, and was fueled by her love for children and a steadfast ambition to get her job done. After her retirement, the community supported Mary by giving her free meals and chatting with her at the saloon. In return, she babysat for many families in the area. Her funeral was reportedly one of the most attended in the town's history.

BELLE STARR

The BANDIT QUEEN

—◆>••<◆—

Born Myra Maybelle Shirley on February 5, 1848, this outlaw lived enough life for an entire generation of women in her short forty-one years. Myra, known as "Belle," grew up in Carthage, Missouri, and received an unusual education for a woman in the mid-1800s. While she attended a girls' academy, as was traditional, she also received a few lessons from her older brother John "Bud" Addison, who was one of her best friends throughout childhood. John taught her everything from how to shoot a gun to how to ride a horse, and their relationship remained strong until his death in 1864, when Belle was sixteen years old. After his death, the Shirley family decided to move to Scyene, Texas, an area in what is now Dallas.

In Scyene, Belle fell into step with a man named Jim Reed, whom she married. The couple had two children, Pearl and Eddie (although there were rumors at the time that Cole Younger of the James-Younger gang may have been Pearl's father). Jim was a nefarious character who often interacted with local lawbreakers. There's no official word or arrest record citing that Belle herself had any involvement with these seedy characters, but many believe she was just as close with them as Jim was. For the believers, there were tales aplenty of Belle riding her horse, Venus, while wearing a velvet skirt and a feathered hat and stealing horses, money, and cattle—and these potentially tall tales earned her the nickname "The Bandit Queen."

Belle and Jim's family spent a lot of time trying to shake their associations with these criminals up until Jim's death in 1874. To make the situation more tense, Belle returned to her family home before her husband died, effectively ending their marriage.

In 1880, Belle married her second husband, Sam Starr, a member of the Starr gang. Sam was Cherokee, and Belle lived with him on Native American land in Oklahoma, where they took part in harboring famous outlaws on the run, like Jesse and Frank James. In a plot twist of sorts, Belle and Sam were arrested and jailed in 1883 for stealing horses and released eighteen months later.

Returning to the Native American territory after her time in prison was an interesting homecoming for Belle. While she was locked up, people talked about her and her crimes. She was said to carry two pistols and wear a gold earring and a feathered hat, a colorful visual for the tall tales starring Belle, which had traveled far past Cherokee territory. But all these legends were exactly that: legends, factless stories.

Belle was brought to trial two more times in her life, but she was never convicted for another crime. It's likely that her reputation preceded her; her husband was still very much involved in crime and gangs, and people naturally assumed she must be involved as well.

After Sam's lifestyle led to his death in 1886, Belle moved on to her last romantic partner, Bill July. Together, they lived on the same Cherokee land, and this time, she refused to have anything to do with the criminals who passed through the area, turning them away if they asked to stay with Belle and Bill. She even had a role in Bill's arrest for horse theft because she didn't defend him when the authorities came to take him away—an attempt to distance herself from a criminal life.

Despite this change of heart, Belle still had her enemies. One was a man named Edgar Watson, who rented land from her. Authorities believe that Belle had sent him packing after learning he was a convicted felon.

On February 3, 1889, right before Belle's forty-first birthday, she was shot dead near Fort Smith, Arkansas. Edgar Watson was taken into custody and questioned about the shooting, but was released, despite having a motive, when police couldn't find any witnesses to the crime. No one has ever been held accountable for her death.

KATE "MA" BARKER

The MOTHER WHO ENCOURAGED HER SONS to COMMIT CRIMES

K ate Barker, born Arizona Donnie Clark, might be most well-known for the way she died. That, and the fact that the villainess in the cult-classic movie *The Goonies* was loosely inspired by her. On January 16, 1935, Kate and her son Fred were gunned down by the FBI in front of their home in a truly massive hail of bullets. Before we get to that part of the story, though, let's start in Springfield, Missouri, in October 1873, the month and year Kate was born.

According to some biographies, Kate spent her childhood going to church, singing, and learning to play the fiddle alongside her siblings. As a child, she also once saw Jesse James and his gang ride through Springfield. Her brush with the infamous James may have been a catalyst for her interest in the Wild West; however, it wasn't until she had children herself that Kate became a full-fledged outlaw.

It's impossible to tell this story without mentioning Kate's family. She had four sons—Herman, Doc, Fred, and Lloyd—with her husband, a farmer named George Barker, and, as the matriarch of the Barker family, she earned the nickname "Ma" Barker. Once her sons were grown, Kate's boys were constantly in and out of jail for crimes ranging from small-time theft to bank robberies. It became too much for George, who couldn't handle Kate's lack of discipline. He left her after the family moved to Tulsa, Oklahoma, in 1915. For sixteen years, the boys continued their crime spree, which culminated in a gruesome two-day rampage in 1931. Fred had just been released on parole from Kansas's Lansing Prison, and had brought one of his fellow inmates, Alvin Karpis, home with him with the intent of looping him into the family crime ring. On the first day of their two-day spree, the group robbed a department store in West Plains, Missouri, and followed that up by shooting the town's sheriff, C. R. Kelly, at point-blank range. There was no motive for this particular killing, and the gang's affinity for senseless violence soon became their trademark.

For Kate's association with her sons' crimes—she provided them with a hideaway house in Tulsa—she became wanted by the police, while her boys continued to commit crimes with various accomplices. Kate was the unifier in these crimes, providing her sons with guidance and approval when they came to her with new opportunities in mind. She had raised them in a religious household, but when they weren't at church, she was teaching them how to become the fearsome criminals they turned into as adults. Aside from robbery, theft, and murder, they also became well-versed in kidnapping. Kate took her sons across the country so they could rob banks and commit petty theft in whichever town they found themselves passing through. During this time, they gained a reputation as the Barker-Karpis Gang, or the Ma Baker Gang. They were regarded as some of the deadliest and most feared people of their time—which makes sense, considering they stole more than $2 million and killed ten people while traveling through the Midwest.

In March 1932, Fred, Alvin, and three additional accomplices robbed the Northwestern National Bank in Minneapolis, stealing more than $250,000 in bonds and cash. Perfect timing brought the family fully together in September 1932 for their most infamous act: the robbery of the Third Northwestern National Bank in Minneapolis. All four of Kate's sons were out of jail, and she gave them the go-ahead, most likely assuming the robbery would be a success, given how well their previous attack had gone. But that confidence was misplaced.

The police were prepared for the crew's arrival, and the robbery attempt ended in a shootout that became near-national news. Everyone made it out alive and none of the gang were arrested, but their notorious reputation only grew, and Kate became even more feared as their leader. For three more years, she lived this life with her sons and their pal Alvin. But in 1935, the FBI managed to track the family's violent conquests all the way down to Florida, where they raided Kate's home in Ocklawaha, a small town north of Orlando. Kate and Fred were in the house when tear gas canisters began flying through the first-floor windows. Fred started shooting his machine gun, but this resulted in a spray of return bullets from the agents outside. Kate fought until she ran out of bullets. The entire shootout lasted four hours, culminating in an eerie silence once both sides' ammunition ran out.

The policemen entered the home to find both Kate and Fred dead in a bedroom on the second floor. One of Kate's arms was gripping a machine gun, while the other was supporting her son.

LAURA "THE THORNY ROSE" BULLION

The LAST SURVIVING MEMBER
of the WILD BUNCH

———◆>••<◆———

Laura Bullion grew up in a family of crime. Laura was raised in Knickerbocker, Texas, by her father, Henry Bullion, a Native American outlaw known for robbing banks, and her mother, Fereby Bullion, the daughter of German immigrants. Laura's parents stayed together for the first five years of her life before splitting up. From there, Fereby and her children moved to live closer to her parents, which also gave Fereby the chance to date again. (You know, grandparents = built-in childcare.)

After Henry died in 1888, Fereby remarried and decided to move away with her new husband, leaving twelve-year-old Laura and her siblings in the care of their grandparents. In other words, Laura's childhood wasn't an easy one. When Laura was fourteen, her aunt, Viana Byler, married William "News" Carver, a train robber who would go on to run with the Black Jack Ketchum Gang but at the time of Laura's childhood was just a cowboy. Carver set up house with Viana, who was seventeen years old at the time.

At the age of fifteen, Laura moved to San Antonio, Texas, where she took up sex work at various bordellos in town. She even spent some time working at the brothel owned by one of the other lawbreaking ladies in this book, Fannie Porter (see page 117). After two years of service, Laura made her way back to Knickerbocker and reentered local society, focusing on her education and community events. But it wasn't long before she went looking for more adventure, and she started by getting to know her uncle William a bit better.

In San Antonio, she had spent some time with William, who by now was a full-fledged outlaw. When Laura moved back home, they continued to correspond through letters, and they remained friends when she left home for the second time to work in dance halls in Texas and Wyoming, where she would eventually meet the infamous Wild Bunch through her uncle. The Wild Bunch gave Laura two nicknames: "Della Rose" and "Thorny Rose"—the latter of which would be immortalized on her gravestone.

In 1901, Laura became quite close with Ben Kilpatrick, a member of the Wild Bunch and former cowboy. He's pictured in the famous "Fort Worth Five" photograph that also showcases Butch Cassidy and the Sundance Kid—the same photo was printed on wanted posters and widely distributed, eventually leading to Ben's arrest. Pressure from the publicity sent Butch Cassidy and the Sundance Kid fleeing to Argentina looking for safer pastures, but Ben stayed in Texas with Laura.

Laura's role in the gang was multifaceted: Some believe she was the lookout during many of their crimes, but her official arrest records state her crime as forgery of signatures on banknotes. On July 3, 1901, the remaining members of the Wild Bunch led another train robbery, targeting the Great Northern Railway, which connected Saint Paul, Minnesota, to Seattle, Washington. The plan was for one of the members to infiltrate the mail car and then force the conductor to stop in Wagner, Minnesota, where two more gang members would board the train and help the first blow open the express car and steal whatever money they could find. They were successful and left the scene of the crime with $83,000 worth of banknotes before splitting up so they could throw the cops off their trail. Laura was involved in the heist, but it's not clear if she was one of the gang members on the train that day. Legend says she served as the lookout, as usual, and helped everyone escape to safety with their money in tow.

Laura and Ben fled to St. Louis, but she was quickly arrested after she was caught forging banknotes. With Laura in custody, authorities were able to locate Ben, though they mistook him for the Sundance Kid. Laura kept her mouth shut, refusing to give up Ben's identity or any details about the train robbery in Wagner. In an attempt to throw off the police, she claimed she had only known Ben, who the police still believed was the Sundance Kid, for a short time. Eventually, Laura was put on trial—as was Ben, when it became clear that he was not the Sundance Kid—and sentenced to five years at the Missouri State Penitentiary. In 1905, three years into her sentence, Laura was released, and her first move was to get closer to Ben, who was doing his time in Atlanta. But although she used the pseudonym Mrs. Freda Arnold, she was still not allowed to visit him in jail.

You can hope for a happy ending for lovebirds Laura and Ben, but you won't find it here. Laura moved to Birmingham, Alabama, having arranged with Ben that he would meet her there after he was released in 1911. As you can probably guess, he never made it. He was arrested for a second time, for murder, in Texas. He was acquitted, but it was just enough to push him back into a life of crime, this time with a man named Ole Hobek. They robbed trains together until 1912, when both were killed while attempting to rob a train in Sanderson, Texas.

Laura chose to live a much quieter life after Ben died, moving to Memphis and changing her name again, this time to Freda Bullion Lincoln. She took up interior design and made draperies to make ends meet, and continued to do this until she died of heart disease on December 2, 1961, around the age of eighty-five, the last surviving member of the Wild Bunch. You can still visit her grave in Memphis's Memorial Park Cemetery, where you'll find three names inscribed on her tombstone: Freda Bullion Lincoln, Laura Bullion, and the Thorny Rose.

PEARL HART

The "LADY BANDIT" of the WILD WEST

———◆>••<◆———

Pearl Hart was a stunning young woman who was brought up in a middle-class family in Toronto. Born in Ontario, Canada, in 1871, she received a respectable education for the time, but when she was just sixteen years old, she fell in love with a young man, and the couple eloped before she had finished her schooling. The marriage became abusive early on, so Pearl left, instead choosing to spend her time with (and affections on) Dan Bandman, a musician who frequented dance halls for performances and a bit of gambling. The new couple moved to Phoenix, Arizona, in 1892, when Pearl was around twenty-one years old.

This is where the story of Pearl the Outlaw really begins. The petite Canadian, who would soon become one of the most legendary Arizona stagecoach robbers, lived quietly until Dan went off to fight in the Spanish–American War. Pearl was quick to find a new partner, though—this time, a drifter named Joe Boot (which was most likely an alias)—and it was a desperate need for money that drove them to commit their first robbery in 1899.

They decided to rob a stagecoach that was traveling between the Arizona towns of Globe and Florence. Pearl showed some generosity at first, stealing $421 from the group on board the coach but returning $1 to each of her victims so they would be able to find something to eat once they arrived at their destination. But Pearl and Joe were not skilled criminals. They did little to cover their tracks or hide their identities from their victims, so they were arrested for the crime just four short days later. Joe landed in a local jail and Pearl was sent to

a prison in Tucson. In Michael Rutter's book *Bedside Book of Bad Girls: Outlaw Women of the American West*, there is an interesting description—as printed in the *Arizona Daily*—of what Pearl was like in prison, according to Sheriff Bill Truman:

> *A tiger cat for verve and endurance. She looks feminine enough now, in the women's clothes I got for her . . . and one can see the touch of a tasteful woman's hand in the way she has brightened up her cell. Yet, only a couple of days ago, I had a struggle with her for my life. She would have killed me in my tracks could she have gotten to her pistol. Sure women are curious creatures.*[1]

In a truly textbook move, Pearl eventually convinced a handful of men to help her escape the prison using her feminine charm. However, her freedom was short-lived, as she was recognized in Deming, New Mexico, and promptly returned to jail in Tucson. (You can't blame a girl for trying!) After she was tried for her act of robbery, both she and Joe were sentenced to thirty years in prison. Neither would serve the full amount of time, though. Pearl was released on December 19, 1902, after becoming pregnant while in prison. To avoid a scandal—the father would have to have been a guard or a fellow prisoner—the governor of the Arizona Territory, Alexander O. Brodie, pardoned her. Joe was released for good behavior a few years after the trial and never showed up in criminal records again.

If I go by historical records, Pearl did the same. It seems that her foray into stagecoach robbery—and the aforementioned prison break—was enough action for the woman who came to be called "The Lady Bandit," among many other nicknames. Of course, there are other ideas about what happened to her after she was pardoned for her crimes. Some say she joined Buffalo Bill's Wild West show and played the role of "The Arizona Bandit." This could have happened.

But it's more likely the pregnant Pearl opted to live a quiet life, leaving her criminal history to simply be a rollicking story for dinner parties and conversation among friends. Or not.

ROSE DUNN

The WOMAN WHO ALLEGEDLY RAN THROUGH BULLETS for LOVE

———⟢••⟤———

Rose Dunn became an outlaw for a man, though she was never arrested or sentenced for any wrongdoing. Like other women in this book, her greatest moments were often in direct opposition to what local authorities would want from a law-abiding citizen, so here we are.

It was George "Bitter Creek" Newcomb who supposedly pulled Rose into a life of crime. Rose was fifteen years old when she first met George in 1893, through two of her five brothers, who had become outlaws associated, like George, with the Wild Bunch. That same year, George and a handful of other gang members were entertaining themselves at George Ransom's saloon—a saloon in Ingalls, Oklahoma—when they were suddenly surrounded by a group of US Marshals. After being directed to step outside and confront the authorities, Bill Doolin's response was, famously, "Go to hell," which set the scene for the epic gunfight to follow.

The following story was never confirmed by Rose or anyone who was in the area at the time of the fight—so take it with a grain of salt. Rose was staying with family in a hotel near the saloon, and it's said that when she heard the confrontation, she grabbed a Winchester rifle, ran out of the hotel through the storm of bullets, and delivered the weapon to her lover, George Newcomb. Another romanticized account claims that from the second floor of the hotel, Rose spotted George struggling with an empty gun chamber, grabbed ammunition, and got it to the lower level of the building by sliding herself down a bedsheet. Like many tales of this time, it's mighty tall. According to Harry Sinclair Drago's book *Outlaws on Horseback*, many locals believe Rose was not even in Ingalls the day of the fight, and that George had his eye on another woman at the hotel.

Drago claims the real Rose was a beautiful, independent girl who often had to dodge the misfortunes her outlaw brothers brought upon themselves. Her stepfather, Dr. W. R. Call, would often warn her when her brothers were up to no good. Nevertheless, she was brought to trial to testify on behalf of the Doolin Gang after the gunfight outside George Ransom's saloon ended in the deaths of some of the marshals on the scene. She was never arrested in relation to this crime.

George's story ends in May 1895, when he stopped by Rose's brothers' home near the Cimarron River to see Rose. With a $5,000 bounty on his head, he was an unfortunate opportunity to make quick money—and Rose's brothers took advantage of it. They ended up turning him in, and George was killed by the local lawmen.

While much of Rose's early story is shrouded in legend, her later years contain less guesswork. After George's death, Rose married a politician in Oklahoma. When Rose herself died, her widower husband had a few words to say about her life as an outlaw: "I first heard her referred to as Rose of Cimarron in 1895, soon after I came down here (to Oklahoma). They called her that, but not because she was a bandit queen. She was a superb horsewoman. She was a true friend of the outlaws and never betrayed them, but she was never the sweetheart of any."[1]

To this day, tales about Rose's involvement with George and the Doolin Gang can't be completely trusted—but they certainly are fun to read.

ETTA PLACE

The QUEEN of the VANISHING ACT

————⟶••⟵————

If you've heard of Etta Place, chances are it was in reference to Harry Alonzo Longabaugh (also known as the Sundance Kid) or Butch Cassidy, but I'm here to tell you this woman was far more than the mere girlfriend of an outlaw.

Many believe that Etta met the Sundance Kid while working at Fannie Porter's brothel in San Antonio. This holds up, as I've already shared that the Wild Bunch used Fannie's bordello as a meeting place of sorts (see page 118). Another important aspect of Etta's life is that no one knew her true first name. Some believe she was a member of Harry's mother's family, as Harry's mother's maiden name was also Place. Others believe she adopted that surname after meeting Harry. There are no official records of Etta's life before she began working in the brothel and the Pinkerton detective agency took interest in her. All this is to reiterate that Etta was a very mysterious character, and it seems that no one knew her basic life details, or they weren't deemed important enough to make official note of. To add to the confusion, some historians believe that Etta Place and Ann Bassett, the girlfriend of another member of the Wild Bunch, were one and the same. While the women do look quite similar in photographs, there is too much conflicting information between their life stories to ever fully prove this theory.

So, while we don't have any definitive facts to rely on, like her birth date, place of birth, or given name, Etta's story is impossible to leave out of this book, considering she pulled off what may be one of the greatest vanishing acts in Wild West history. With that in mind, maybe the lack of detail around her life was intentional. Etta had something in common with fellow outlaw Laura Bullion, as she was one of five women allowed to visit Robbers Roost, the Wild Bunch's hideout in Utah. Etta had a direct in with Butch Cassidy—according to some legends, she became his eventual mistress. This relationship, whatever degree it might have been, linked her with the Wild Bunch.

One crime in particular sent Etta, Butch, and Harry fleeing the country to throw the authorities off their trail. They moved to Argentina, and eventually ended up in Chile, living life on the run for a year before Etta was hit with a bout of homesickness and returned to California, traveling with Harry from Valparaíso, Chile, to San Francisco in June 1906. After Etta was settled back in the United States, Harry returned to Chile to rejoin Butch. Butch and Harry allegedly died together in a gunfight with South American authorities in Bolivia on November 7, 1908, although their bodies were never identified, which has led some to doubt the truth of their demise.

Despite this, Etta lived on—the only problem is, no one knows where or how. She was last documented in San Francisco at some point in 1907. From there, she very literally disappears from records. Given how determined the detectives at Pinkerton were to capture the Wild Bunch and the fact that they had previous descriptions of and information on Etta, it's hard to believe she simply vanished. And if that really is the case, then what a feat that would have been. Either way, it's fun to imagine she has grandchildren somewhere, telling stories of their grandmother and her outlaw friends.

LILLIAN SMITH

ANNIE OAKLEY'S GUNSLINGING RIVAL

—❖••❖—

Lillian Smith was an interesting character. Half her infamy comes from her cocky attitude as Annie Oakley's rival gunslinger, and the other half comes from an act of appropriation that would have gotten her canceled her so fast in modern culture, her head would spin. Lillian was a was a brazen sharpshooter who transgressed Victorian gender norms. But after challenging Annie Oakley one too many times, Lillian, a white Mormon, also began playing the role of a Sioux markswoman in a traveling Wild West show. Before we dig into that mess, let's start with her stiff rivalry.

Many people have heard of Annie Oakley, the American exhibition shooter who made headlines at the age of fifteen for beating Frank E. Butler, a traveling-show marksman, in a shooting match. (Fun fact: She later married him!) But Lillian was also a teenage star, grabbing people's attention after her first shooting competition at the age of ten. Her father offered a $5,000 bet that no one could beat her, including the famous Doc Carver (who never showed up to their match). In 1886, at the age of fifteen, Lillian joined Buffalo Bill Cody's Wild West show—the very same show Annie Oakley was headlining. This was Lillian's first time in the spotlight, and she was billed by the show as the "California Girl," according to Julia Bricklin's book *America's Best Female Sharpshooter: The Rise and Fall of Lillian Frances Smith*.

Both women were familiar with competing against men, so it was interesting that they were each other's first female opponents. In a different world, they might have become friends, but Lillian's haughty attitude and ego—she was often overheard trash-talking Annie—quickly built a wall between them. This tension drew in crowds to see the two women compete while technically playing on the same team.

In 1887, the two shooters performed in front of Queen Victoria. While both Annie and Lillian showed up to the exhibition and had flawless performances, the press was tougher on Annie, calling out that the prince shook Lillian's hand ahead of Annie's. This act was translated as the prince putting Lillian's success ahead of Annie's, and it may have been enough to kick Annie's competitive edge into hyperdrive. Shortly after, Lillian had a poor showing at the Wimbledon rifle competition in London, and the British newspapers took notice. All Annie had to do to regain her spotlight was show up a few days later and perform better than Lillian—but it wasn't enough to keep her on the roster at the Wild West show. Buffalo Bill had been talking up Lillian more than Annie at the time, so Annie made the decision to leave the show.

Lillian's lackluster performance at Wimbledon followed her back home, despite Bill's encouragement and public support. Many media outlets criticized the British newspapers for portraying Lillian in such a polished, intellectual light. She was known in the Wild West for her coarse way with words, and back in the US, she was mocked mercilessly for her London showing. As all this was happening, Lillian was also accused of cheating during her Wild West show shoots, a scandal that culminated in Lillian leaving the show . . . and Annie returning in 1889. This wasn't a coincidence: Annie had demanded Lillian's removal from the show as part of her agreement to return. Around this time, Lillian's marriage to Jim "Kidd" Willoughby, a cowboy twelve years her senior, fell apart. He continued to tour with the show even after Lillian was kicked out. In an attempt to keep her fame after she left the show, Lillian challenged Annie to a match, which Annie declined, and for a while after that, Lillian disappeared.

Lillian may have lost Jim's admiration, but she quickly remarried, this time to Charles "Frank" Hafley, who owned a saloon in Santa Cruz. As soon as she met Charles—a sheriff for Tulare County, California, at the time—she was smitten. They first laid eyes on each other at a gallery in Visalia, California, in 1898, and began a relationship that spanned a full decade.

With a taste of fame in her system, Lillian found another way to stay top of mind. She and Charles formed their own show called California Frank's Wild West. In their traveling show, Lillian played the role of Princess Wenona, a sharpshooting Native American teenager. Charles was "Fighting Frank," who whisked Wenona away to the modern world. In addition to the show, they created a collection of alleged "Native American" curios—an exhibit of objects framed as rare or unusual—which included a line of tomahawks Lillian designed.

Lillian and Charles's show was a mix of physical feats of agility and strength, as well as a love story of sorts. Lillian even loved the Native American costumes so much, she became known for wearing the outfits outside of performances (which would be considered a major no-no today). A great book by Angela Pulley Hudson called *Real Native Genius: How an Ex-Slave and a White Mormon Became Famous Indians* dives into the public's appreciation—and destruction—of Native American communities during the late 1800s, and describes how Lillian was far from the only person to appropriate Native American culture at the time. Her performances actually started the trend of featuring Native American "princess" characters in other Wild West shows; her younger sister, Nellie Smith, had a princess act of her own.

There isn't any official story or information about what happened between Lillian and Charles that resulted in the end of their marriage, but in 1925, Lillian met Emil Lenders, a famous painter of American landscapes, and fell in love. Emil helped Lillian transition from a life onstage to a quiet way of living among like-minded people. Together, they moved into a home on a ranch in Ponca City, Oklahoma. But in 1928, Emil left Lillian to marry another woman, and she never fell in love again.

She moved into a cabin near the same ranch she had shared with Emil, where she lived with lots of dogs. But after just a year on her own, she developed a heart disorder. Once she knew she wasn't getting any healthier, in true Lillian fashion, she asked her remaining friends to bury her in one of her show costumes. At the age of fifty-nine, Lillian died, and her friends followed through on their promise.

BONNIE PARKER

YOU KNOW, *THAT* BONNIE

———◆>••<◆———

I f somehow you've never heard the names "Bonnie and Clyde" before, or seen the classic eponymous film, then strap in for this wild story.

Bonnie Parker was nineteen when she met Clyde Barrow in 1930. At the time, she was married—her husband was in jail for murder—but that didn't stop her from pursuing things with Clyde. Soon after they met, Clyde, too, was sent to jail . . . only to escape shortly after with a gun Bonnie had smuggled in for him. His freedom was short-lived (he was re-captured), though, because in February 1932, Clyde was released on parole and the couple began their life as car-stealing outlaws. In 1932, they stuck mainly to Texas, robbing people and businesses and leaving the occasional casualty, and they stole what they needed to get by: food, gas, cash. According to *Smithsonian* magazine, Bonnie eventually felt comfortable enough in her robbing abilities to ditch her flat running shoes for a pair of high heels.[1]

But on April 13, 1933, things escalated for the criminal couple. Bonnie and Clyde—along with their frequent partner in crime and un-official photographer, W. D. Jones—were in Joplin, Missouri, visiting with Clyde's brother, Buck, and sister-in-law, Blanche. The police had set up a raid of Buck and Blanche's home under the hunch that they were running a bootlegging operation, but uncovered much, much more. Of course, the group's reaction was to draw their guns. At the end of it all, two officers were dead, and Bonnie, Clyde, Buck, Blanche, and W. D. got out just fine—but the incident lit a fire under their tails. In the span of one night, Clyde drove them 600 miles to Shamrock, Texas, to escape the attention. From there, they continued on their travels, driving through Missouri, Arkansas, and Oklahoma for three months, stealing cars and swapping license plates along the way to throw the police off their tracks. Bonnie acted as the navigator, directing Clyde from the passenger seat of whatever car they were driving that day.

Before the botched raid on Buck and Blanche's home, Bonnie's name wasn't known throughout Texas, but that quickly changed after photos the police had found during the raid in Joplin were published in local papers. Almost overnight, Bonnie became the talk of many towns. Together, she and Clyde also became a sex symbol of sorts: two thrill-seeking criminals traveling together . . . unmarried. Scandalous! But their newfound celebrity made it hard for them to travel unnoticed, let alone commit the petty robberies they came to rely on to survive.

In February 1934—four short years after Bonnie and Clyde met—the state of Texas enlisted Frank Hamer, a former Texas Ranger, to hunt down the notorious duo. And that he did. Armed with information from a family member of the Barrow Gang, he eventually cornered the couple on May 23, 1934, near Gibsland, Louisiana. In what might be their most infamous move, Bonnie and her man, Clyde, drove the Ford sedan they had stolen directly into the rain of the police's gunfire, resulting in both of their deaths.

Bonnie was twenty-three when she died, and her mother said that she believed a majority of grievers came to see Bonnie's body at the couple's shared funeral, which brought in an estimated ten thousand visitors. Of all the women in this book, there isn't one who is more remembered than Bonnie. Her spectacularly bold and gruesome final act still lives on today in movies, books, and cultural references.

MARIE BAKER

"*The* PRETTY PANTS BANDIT"

T his is a short tale, but it's about possibly the most inventive criminal in this book—so enjoy.

Every outlaw needs a signature move, and Marie Baker, later revealed to be Rose Durante after her arrest, had a very particular way of throwing off her victims. Her nickname, "The Pretty Pants Bandit," all but gives it away.

In 1933, Marie and her gang committed a handful of robberies in Miami. For a year, she traveled around the city, toting two guns at a time, demanding money from shop employees. She got her infamous nickname from the most vital part of her crime: demanding that the person she was stealing from drop their pants as she left the area. Her cry of "Take off your pants!" was a serious one. If anyone didn't

immediately follow her direction, she would help them with the act. The result was disarmingly successful, to say the least.

Something about the way Marie was captured just . . . makes sense. While robbing a butcher shop in the same string of crimes, she took a moment to fix her makeup in a reflective surface. While she was doing so, one of her hostages escaped and alerted the local authorities. Marie was arrested on the spot, and soon her real identity was revealed. She served time for her crimes, but no one is sure what happened to her after she was released. This is the perfect kind of criminal: inventive, mysterious, and wildly visual—I can't help but imagine her giggling her jail days away over the shocked faces her victims sported after hearing her request.

REABLE CHILDS AND THE GOREE GIRLS

The WOMEN WHO SANG THEIR WAY OUT *of* PRISON

————◆>••<◆————

When you think of famous female country musicians, your brain is most likely thousands of miles away from naming this group of prisoners. But that's exactly what this group of bandits, murderers, and other criminals at Goree State Farm, just outside Huntsville, Texas—the only prison for women in the state at the time—came to be.

The women who made up the Goree All Girl String Band were

Mozelle McDaniel (in jail for attempted murder), Reable Childs (murder), Ruby Mae Morace (robbery), Georgia Fay Collins (burglary), Ruby Dell Guyton (cattle rustling), Bonnie Scott (robbery), Lillie Mae Dudley (assault and robbery), and Burma Harris (possession of heroin). The band became a national musical sensation, which resulted in lengthy lines of adoring fans looking for autographs, marriage proposals, and a ton of mail sent to the prison with the hopes that the "Goree Girls," as they came to be known, would see it. The catalyst for this band coming together, however, arguably originated from an even more unexpected place: a fellow prison a few miles away in Huntsville, Texas, that housed male criminals.

In March 1938, the radio show *Thirty Minutes Behind the Walls*, which took listeners into the Texas penitentiary's Huntsville Unit (nicknamed the Walls Unit), premiered. As opposed to the "behind the scenes" reality television we know today, the weekly program, broadcast on Wednesdays at ten thirty p.m., was dedicated to giving both male and female inmates space to perform—music, mainly. The overarching goal was to showcase a prison beaten down by bad press in a more human-focused light. As it turns out, an incredibly well-received appearance on the program paved the way to opportunity for the group of aforementioned women at Goree State Farm. They became regulars on the show after their first appearance, and were often requested by their adoring fans, and Reable Childs, the founding member of the group, encouraged the other members to take the act seriously.

Childs's story will make you cringe. If you're looking for the quick version: Childs married a man who did not want to have children. After her husband denied her a divorce, she found solace in a raging affair with another local man, who eventually murdered Childs's husband by shooting him with a .22-caliber shotgun through a window in their home. Childs never confessed to the murder (her fling did), but she was handed a twenty-five-year sentence after a highly publicized trial. The reasoning? The jury believed she had *lured* the man into an evil union. Okay, feel the cringe, be the cringe, and let it pass. Back to the larger story.

Childs believed that finding success as a band would get her and the other girls out of Goree. One of her bandmates, Mozelle McDaniel, shared as much in an interview with *Texas Monthly* in May 2003: "Reable said we could sing our way out of Goree. Sure did. Said we didn't have to live like this . . . She said we could be better than those men. That's what she said."[1]

There was something about these criminal women doing something so beautiful and entertaining that captured the hearts of people around the country, and by 1944, all but one of the original band members had received early parole. Once released, the women faded into normal lives. The band had served its purpose.

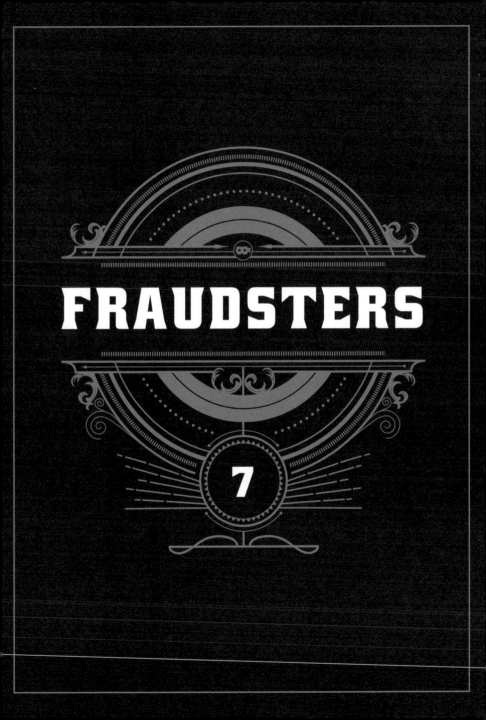

ALL WAS NOT WHAT IT SEEMED

People lie every day. But there is a massive difference between a person who will never reveal their true age and a person who is constantly changing their name in an effort to steal or borrow money they will never repay.

In this section, I'll introduce you to some women who made their own marks on history by lying their way into the newspaper headlines.

Terms to Know

Séance: A meeting held with the intent of communicating or interacting with the dead, led by a medium or someone who claims to have a direct line of communication with those who have passed.

Spiritualism: A system of belief or religious practice based on supposed communication with the spirits of the dead, especially through mediums.

Calling card: A card bearing a person's name and address, often showcasing their achievements or important life details, sent or left in lieu of a formal social call or business visit.

Clairvoyant: A person who claims to have a supernatural ability to perceive events in the future or beyond normal sensory contact.

Promissory note: A signed document containing a written promise to pay a stated sum to a specified person or the bearer at a specified date or on demand.

Honorably discharged: To be released from military service with a favorable record.

Buffalo soldiers: Nickname given by Native American tribes to soldiers in the African American cavalry regiments of the United States Army in the nineteenth century, who patrolled the western frontier following the Civil War.

PRINCESS CARABOO

The EXOTIC STRANGER
WHO WAS *a* COMPLETE FRAUD

———◆>••<◆———

T he story of Princess Caraboo appears to come straight from a movie plot. In April 1817, a woman seemingly washed ashore in Almondsbury in Gloucestershire, England, where, properly confused, she stumbled across a cobbler. The cobbler wasn't quite sure what to do with this stranger, who spoke an unknown language and was dressed in unfamiliar clothing, but eventually sent her to the local overseer of the poor to determine whether she was a vagrant. The overseer passed her along to Samuel Worrall, the county magistrate, to see if he or his American-born wife could translate the woman's words. They could not, so the woman was deemed a beggar and sent to the workhouse in neighboring Bristol. While she was imprisoned, however, a Portuguese sailor learned of her predicament and felt confident that he could translate the strange woman's words. And as it turns out, what she had to say was astonishing.

According to the sailor's translation, the woman identified herself as Princess Caraboo from an island called Javasu in the Indian Ocean. As her story went, pirates had captured her at sea, and as they approached the Bristol Channel, she saw an opportunity to jump overboard and swim to shore—washing up in Almondsbury, where we began this story. Given the grandeur and adventure of her tale, locals ate her story up. Samuel Worrall and his wife subsequently invited Princess Caraboo to come stay with them in their home, where they used her as an attraction of sorts, showing off her use of a bow and arrow, her prayers to the god "Allah Tallah," her fencing skills, and her affinity for nude swimming. They even discovered strange marks on the back of her head, which a local doctor thought were the result of a style of cupping used in Asia.

The exotic-stranger act lasted for a while, until someone recognized the woman's sketch in the *Bristol Journal*. As it happened, she wasn't a princess from a faraway island at all—in fact, the island of Javasu was entirely fictional. She was the daughter of a cobbler from Witheridge, Devon, another small village in England—seventy miles away from Almondsbury.

Princess Caraboo's real name was Mary Willcocks, and she had worked as a servant all over England before making up her new persona and giving it a go in Almondsbury. Her reason? She simply wanted to make her life a little more interesting. Instead of painting her as the town's least favorite person, the press played up her fraudulence as the victory of a poor woman against the aristocratic, fooling those in the highest level of society.

The press's depiction of Mary's deceit helped her make the next move. Given her newfound and entirely unlikely popularity, she was able to raise funds to relocate, with help from Mrs. Worrall, who had shown empathy to Mary throughout her extravagant deception and supported Mary through her fund-raising. Eventually, Mary had enough money to travel to Philadelphia. After her arrival in the city in June 1817, she turned her character of Princess Caraboo into a stage show, eventually taking the production north to New York City. After seven years in the United States, and a small amount of success, she returned to England, taking her show to London, but the interest in her tall tale had dissipated. Eventually, she lost her connection to the Worralls. She did marry a man named Robert Baker, though, with whom she had a daughter. A UK census taken in the late 1820s placed Mary in Bristol, England, selling leeches to the local hospital to get by. She died of a heart attack in 1864.

LEAH, KATE, AND MAGGIE FOX

The SPIRITUAL SISTERS

I n March 1848, an incident occurred that would forever change the lives of the Fox sisters—Leah, Catherine (Kate), and Margaretta (Maggie). The entire family—including the girls' parents, Margaret and John—had been hearing a series of heavy rapping noises in the same place every night as soon as they had gone to bed. The young girls began asking questions and directing the source of the knocking to respond. John and Margaret, even more curious, began to investigate the sounds. Their search was fruitless, at least when it came to living suspects. After hunting through the house for the source of the knocking and withstanding nights without sleep due to the unsettling sounds, the family determined it was the spirit of the previous occupant answering their queries by knocking on the wall.

The Fox home in Hydesville, near Rochester, New York, quickly became well-known for this paranormal activity, and strangers started showing up at the house asking to witness the knocking. Here's the catch—and I'm sorry to ruin any of your hopes that this was going to be a *true* ghost story: The sisters were behind the mysterious noises. Leah, the eldest sister, soon recognized the potential in their situation and set up organized viewings of her sisters' communications with the "spirit." Kate and Maggie were pegged as mediums by the general public and those who witnessed the call-and-response sessions, all of whom were convinced the sisters could communicate with the spirit. This phenomenon became known as the "Rochester Rappings."

The three sisters moved to New York City in 1850 to further show off their "gift" and found lucrative opportunities to demonstrate their skills. The media wholeheartedly believed the women and widely publicized their séances. The Fox sisters were responsible for much more than a few private events, though: They played a huge role in the beginnings of the spiritualism trend of the era and the concept of communicating with the dead. Many other supposed "mediums" followed, some quickly being outed as fakes, but the craze of spiritualism raged on.

The sisters spent the rest of their lives facing different realities. Kate dove headfirst into spiritualism, setting up the Society for the Diffusion of Spiritual Knowledge, which sponsored free séances for the public. As her name grew in popularity, her communication methods also grew. Her séances often incorporated music, writing, and materializations, or alleged physical manifestations of the spirits being contacted.

Leah stayed put in New York and continued to host séances. There seemed to be a distance between Leah and her sisters, and sources say that she would later chastise Kate for her drinking habit as well as accuse her of being a bad mother to her children.

Maggie ended up meeting the explorer Elisha Kent Kane, who urged her to give up spiritualism and seek out a path of education. She listened to him, ultimately converting to Roman Catholicism in 1858. It wasn't until after his death, though, that Maggie shared she had been Elisha's common-law wife and published the love letters he had written to her.

In a letter published in the *New York World* on October 21, 1888, Maggie confessed that the original rappings in the Fox sisters' childhood home had been fake, a prank she had pulled with Kate in order to scare their mother. Many chose not to believe her confession, and she eventually attempted to retract the statement herself. But the damage had been done.

Both Maggie and Kate eventually descended into alcoholism, and their lives ended in poverty. Leah died in 1890, having never reconciled with Maggie after she publicly outed the sisters' scam.

CATHAY WILLIAMS

The DARING BUFFALO SOLDIER

There's one thing you'll want to keep in mind throughout this story: In the mid-1800s, it was illegal for a woman to serve in the US Army. But Cathay Williams, who was born into slavery, did just this in 1866 when, under the name William Cathay, she enlisted as a member of the 38th Infantry Regiment—a unit that would eventually become a small part of the historic buffalo soldiers, the African American cavalry regiments who served following the Civil War.

Enlisting as a soldier actually wasn't her first introduction to the army: Cathay was previously pressed into service as a washerwoman and cook for the Union Army. But when she decided to become a soldier, it was relatively easy, given that recruits were not required to undergo a full medical exam at the time, and it wasn't until years later that Cathay was revealed to be a woman.

But let's start at the beginning: Cathay enlisted for three years of active duty. Before getting too far into her term, she contracted smallpox and was sent to a hospital in East St. Louis, Illinois. Smallpox treatment did not require a full medical exam, so her sex was not discovered during her stay. She was discharged and sent back into service in New Mexico, but the side effects of the smallpox continued to put a strain on her body. Eventually, a number of injuries and exhaustion landed her back in the hospital, this time with a surgeon who performed a more detailed exam to diagnose Cathay's issues and ended up blasting her secret to smithereens.

The surgeon went to Captain Charles E. Clarke to share the news, and subsequently, Cathay was honorably discharged from the army—specifically, she received a "disability discharge"—on October 14, 1868. But her career as a soldier was far from done.

After her discharge, she began working as a cook at Fort Union in New Mexico, and later moved to Pueblo, Colorado. She was married in Colorado, but her relationship dissolved after her husband robbed her and stole a team of horses. Cathay didn't let him off the hook: She had him arrested. Later, she moved eighty-five miles south to a town called Trinidad, Colorado, where she found work as a seamstress and began a new life.

From then on out, her days were much quieter, compared to her early life. She spent the rest of them fighting for disability payments from the army, having been diagnosed with diabetes and neuralgia, but was denied time and time again. While she was living in Trinidad, a reporter from the *St. Louis Daily Times* heard about her legacy and interviewed her for a story narrating her heroic lifetime, which ran in the newspaper on January 2, 1876. Cathay's specific day of death is unknown, but her legacy as the only female buffalo soldier lives on in history books and celebrations of women who chose the path much less traveled.

ELIZABETH BIGLEY

The FRAUD WHO NEVER LEARNED HER LESSON

———◆>••<◆———

The first time Elizabeth Bigley was arrested, she was thirteen years old. Her plan was exceptionally beyond her years and only foreshadowed her deceitful future: The teenager tricked a bank into sending her legitimate checks under the ruse that her uncle had passed away and left her a sum of money. The checks let her spend the money ahead of gaining official access to the bank account, which did not exist. After a few months, her ploy was discovered; Elizabeth was arrested and told never to do something like that again. The consequence was a slap on the wrist. She didn't listen.

Elizabeth grew up to become a queen of lies—and many aliases, a method of disguise she used to create new identities in order to scam people out of their hard-earned money. Her most well-known move was presenting checks to business owners exceeding the amount of her purchase and asking for the difference in cash. If she was ever questioned about the amount of money on the check, she was prepared. Elizabeth had sent a letter to herself, bearing the fictitious name and address of an attorney in Ontario, which alerted her to the fact that she had become the heiress of $15,000 after the death of a philanthropist. To make it seem even more legitimate, she had calling cards made announcing her inheritance. She would show these calling cards to the shop owners, who bought the story hook, line, and sinker. She was only twenty-two years old when she created this scheme—but it would come back to haunt her.

Elizabeth ended up moving to Cleveland to live with her sister, Alice, and Alice's husband, with the promise that she wouldn't stay long and would soon launch her own life. In reality, Elizabeth was exploring their home while they were out during the day and assigning a value to all the furniture and other décor in the house. She then went to the bank to take out a loan using her sister's possessions as collateral. Alice's husband caught on to what Elizabeth was doing and promptly kicked her out of their home, but Elizabeth had already moved on to her next victim.

Shortly after leaving Alice's, she met Dr. Wallace S. Springsteen, introducing herself to the doctor with a new first name, Lydia. They married on November 21, 1883 . . . and divorced twelve days later, after a number of indebted shop owners saw the marriage announcement in the Cleveland *Plain Dealer* and demanded repayment for Elizabeth's false checks. Her husband paid off the debts to save his own line of credit, but dissolved the marriage in return.

From that moment on, Elizabeth, alias Lydia, was constantly reinventing herself. She took on different names: She was Madam Marie Rosa, the clairvoyant niece of famous Civil War general William Tecumseh Sherman. She ended up marrying two of her clients, one marriage short-lived (not much is known about this union) and the other to a businessman named G. L. Hoover, with whom she had a child and who left her his $50,000 estate after his death. With the money, she moved herself and her son to Toledo, Ohio, and reinvented herself once more.

She continued her "work" as a clairvoyant under the name Madame Devere, gaining a client who paid her $10,000 to act as his financial adviser. Elizabeth would ask this client, a man named Joseph Lamb, to cash checks for her so she wouldn't have to travel across the state to access her personal account. She milked $40,000 from the false checks he cashed, and they were both arrested once the bank caught on. Eventually Joseph was acquitted of the crimes and deemed a victim in Elizabeth's scam. She was sentenced to nearly ten years in jail, but was able to get an early release after writing letters to the parole board with promises to change.

With her freedom in hand, Elizabeth moved on to perhaps her most grand act of deception. Once again, she caught the eye of a wealthy man—this time, Leroy S. Chadwick, who knew her by the name of Cassie L. Hoover. Leroy was a rich widower and a member of one of the oldest families in Cleveland. She moved into his home, bringing along her son, Emil. Once settled, she wasted no time in getting to know the wealthy neighbors along Euclid Avenue. She quickly became known for spending top dollar on everything she purchased— jewelry dripping in gems, artwork from around the world, extravagant furniture. She also continued her habit of taking out bank loans, paying for one with the funds from another. Elizabeth was passing out forged promissory notes—most commonly from her father, who she claimed was Andrew Carnegie—and accepting personal checks from investment bankers. One of these bankers, Herbert Newton, eventually realized she would never repay him the $104,000 he had ended up loaning her and took the situation to court in November 1904. Even Andrew Carnegie attended the trial, and examined the promissory notes that Elizabeth had forged in his name, debunking them and pointing out their many spelling errors.

Elizabeth was sentenced to ten years in jail for conspiracy to defraud a national bank. It's estimated that the haul from her lifetime of fraud would be worth upward of $16.5 million today.

ACKNOWLEDGMENTS

I am ever thankful for the support of my family—Dan, Jeanne, and Ryan—for listening to me talk about this project to no end and for enduring my late-night calls when I just needed a friendly voice. I love you all.

The most massive of thank-yous to my editor, Lauren Hummel, who continues to guide me through the writing process with grace. I cannot begin to tell you how your thoughtful edits and words of encouragement have helped me grow.

The stories of these women have filled my dreams since I started reading into them. For that, I have many fellow authors to thank who have put together books, articles, and shared historical photos of these lawbreaking ladies. There's no shortage of drama, and for that I am thankful . . . that I didn't cross some of these women in real life.

Lastly, a big hug to my local library for answering my every question about their e-book system and providing me with more reading material than I could have ever imagined.

BIBLIOGRAPHY

SAYYIDA AL-HURRA
Favilli, Elena. *Good Night Stories for Rebel Girls: 100 Tales of Extraordinary Women*. Los Angeles: Timbuktu Labs, Inc., 2016.

Porath, Jason. *Rejected Princesses: Tales of History's Boldest Heroines, Hellions, and Heretics*. New York: Dey Street Books, 2016.

JACQUOTTE "BACK FROM THE DEAD RED" DELAHAYE
Favilli, Elena. *Good Night Stories for Rebel Girls: 100 Tales of Extraordinary Women*. Los Angeles: Timbuktu Labs, Inc., 2016.

INGELA GATHENHIELM
Duncombe, Laura Sook. *A Pirate's Life for She: Swashbuckling Women Through the Ages*. Chicago: Chicago Review Press, 2019.

ANNE BONNY
Bartelme, Tony. "The True and False Stories of Anne Bonny, Pirate Woman of the Caribbean." *Post and Courier*, November 21, 2018. https://www.postandcourier.com/news/the-true-and-false-stories-of-anne-bonny-pirate-woman/article_e7fc1e2c-101d-11e8-90b7-9fdf20ba62f8.html.

Encyclopaedia Britannica Online, s.v. "Anne Bonny." Accessed June 26, 2019. https://www.britannica.com/biography/Anne-Bonny.

Porath, Jason. *Rejected Princesses: Tales of History's Boldest Heroines, Hellions, and Heretics*. New York: Dey Street Books, 2016.

Tucker, Phillip Thomas. *Anne Bonny the Infamous Female Pirate*. Port Townsend, WA: Feral House, 2017.

RACHEL WALL
Duncombe, Laura Sook. *A Pirate's Life for She: Swashbuckling Women Through the Ages*. Chicago: Chicago Review Press, 2019.

National Parks Service. "Rachel Wall, Pirate." U.S. Department of the Interior. Accessed March 4, 2020. https://www.nps.gov/people/rachel-wall.htm.

CHING SHIH
Porath, Jason. *Rejected Princesses: Tales of History's Boldest Heroines, Hellions, and Heretics*. New York: Dey Street Books, 2016.

Sarkeesian, Anita, and Ebony Adams. *History vs. Women: The Defiant*

BIBLIOGRAPHY

Lives That They Don't Want You to Know. New York: Feiwel and Friends, 2018.

SADIE "THE GOAT" FARRELL

Legends of America. "Sadie 'The Goat' Farrell." Accessed March 4, 2020. https://www.legendsofamerica.com/ny-sadiefarrell/.

Sparber, Max. *Sadie the Goat*. United States: Independently published, 2019.

MARIA GERTRUDIS "LA TULES" BARCELÓ

Encyclopaedia Britannica Online. s.v. "Gertrudis Barceló." Accessed January 1, 2020. https://www.britannica.com/biography/Gertrudis -Barcelo.

ELEANOR "MADAME MOUSTACHE" DUMONT

Enss, Chris. *The Lady Was a Gambler: True Stories of Notorious Women of the Old West*. Guilford, CT: Globe Pequot, 2007.

Legends of America. "Eleanor Dumont." Accessed March 4, 2020. https:// www.legendsofamerica.com/we-eleanoredumont/.

BELLE SIDDONS

"A Beautiful Wretch." *Omaha Daily Bee*, October 10, 1881. https:// chroniclingamerica.loc.gov/lccn/sn99021999/1881-10-10/ed-1/seq -7/#date1=1836&sort=date&date2=1922&searchType=advanced&langu age=&sequence=0&index=0&words=Madame Vestal&proxdistance=5&s tate=&rows=20&ortext=&proxtext=&phrasetext=Madam Vestal&andtex t=&dateFilterType=yearRange&page=1.

Koller, Joe. "Famed Deadwood Faro Queen Turned War Spy Talents Over to Highwaymen." *Rapid City Journal*, February 21, 2005. https:// rapidcityjournal.com/travel/famed-deadwood-faro-queen-turned-war- spy-talents-over-to/article_658c4156-e0a8-5608-8625-bc6bf9368 5c1.html.

LOTTIE DENO

Enss, Chris. *The Lady Was a Gambler: True Stories of Notorious Women of the Old West*. Guilford, CT: Globe Pequot, 2007.

Enss, Chris. "Wild Women of the West: Lottie Deno." *Cowgirl*, June 27, 2018. https://cowgirlmagazine.com/wild-women-lottie-deno/.

Legends of America. "Lottie Deno: Queen of the Paste Board Flappers." Accessed March 4, 2020. https://www.legendsofamerica.com/we -lottiedeno/.

Rose, Cynthia. *Lottie Deno: Gambling Queen of Hearts*. Santa Fe, NM: Clear Light Publishers, 1994.

"POKER ALICE" TUBBS

Boswell, Evelyn. "Miners Faced Rough Times in Early American West." MSU

BIBLIOGRAPHY

News Service, Montana State University, April 30, 2007. https://www
.montana.edu/news/4838/miners-faced-rough-times-in-early-american
-west.

Denver Public Library. "'Poker' Alice Tubbs (1851–1930)." December 31, 2018.
https://history.denverlibrary.org/colorado-biographies/poker-alice
-tubbs-1851-1930.

Enss, Chris. *The Lady Was a Gambler: True Stories of Notorious Women
of the Old West.* Guilford, CT: Globe Pequot, 2007.

Mumey, Nolie. *Poker Alice: Alice Ivers Duffield Tubbs Huckert, 1851–
1930; History of a Woman Gambler in the West.* Denver: Artcraft
Press, 1951.

STEPHANIE ST. CLAIR
Stewart, Shirley Pamela. *The World of Stephanie St. Clair: An Entrepre-
neur, Race Woman and Outlaw in Early Twentieth Century Harlem.*
New York: Peter Lang, 2014.

Watson, Elwood. "Stephanie St. Clair (1897–1969)." BlackPast.org, February
13, 2008. https://www.blackpast.org/african-american-history/st-clair
-stephanie-1886-1969/.

JUDY BAYLEY
Schwartz, David. "My Nevada 5: Exceptional Women in Gaming." News
Center, University of Nevada, Las Vegas, June 3, 2014. Accessed March
4, 2020. https://www.unlv.edu/news/article/my-nevada-5-exceptional
-women-gaming.

Taylor, F. Andrew. "Judy Bayley Was Philanthropist, Businesswoman." *Las
Vegas Review-Journal.* January 7, 2014. https://www.reviewjournal
.com/local/local-las-vegas/downtown/judy-bayley-was-philanthropist
-businesswoman/.

MARY LOUISE CECILIA "TEXAS" GUINAN
Encyclopaedia Britannica Online, s.v. "Texas Guinan." Accessed January 8, 2020. https://www.britannica.com/biography/Texas-Guinan.

"Queens of the Speakeasies." Mob Museum, n.d. Accessed March 4, 2020.
http://prohibition.themobmuseum.org/the-history/the-prohibition
-underworld/queens-of-the-speakeasies/.

Trachtenberg, Leo. "Texas Guinan: Queen of the Night." *City Journal.*
Spring 1998. https://www.city-journal.org/html/texas-guinan-queen
-night-11938.html.

WILLIE CARTER SHARPE
Casey, Dan. "'The Wettest Spot on Earth': Moonshine, a Virginia County and a
Trial that Captivated the Nation." *Richmond Times-Dispatch,* June 17,
2018. https://www.richmond.com/zzstyling/disco-rich-body/the-wet

test-spot-on-earth-moonshine-a-virginia-county-and/article_8c89bd6d
-f5ba-5267-801c-dc525778e4f7.html.

Thompson, Charles D. *Spirits of Just Men: Mountaineers, Liquor Bosses, and Lawmen in the Moonshine Capital of the World*. Champaign, IL: University of Illinois Press, 2011.

Toppo, Greg. "'Moonshine' Tracks Centuries-Old U.S. Whiskey Trail." *USA Today*, July 18, 2014. https://www.usatoday.com/story/life /books/2014/07/18/moonshine-book-history/12805851/.

MAGGIE BAILEY

Block, Melissa. "'Queen of the Mountain Bootleggers' Maggie Bailey." *All Things Considered*, NPR, December 8, 2005. https://www.npr.org /templates/story/story.php?storyId=5044685.

MARY WAZENIAK

"The Battle over Booze." *Chicago Tribune*, July 25, 2014. http://galleries .apps.chicagotribune.com/chi-prohibition-chicago-20140725-photos/.

Grygo, John. "The Hidden History of Women Bootleggers." UNLV Public History, University of Nevada, Las Vegas, November 4, 2016. https://www .unlvpublichistory.com/the-hidden-history-of-women-bootleggers.

Joyce, Jaime. *Moonshine: A Cultural History of America's Infamous Liquor*. New York: Zenith Press, 2014.

GLORIA DE CASARES

Minnick, Fred. *Whiskey Women: The Untold Story of How Women Saved Bourbon, Scotch, Irish Whiskey*. Lincoln, NE: Potomac Books, 2013.

"Overstays Her Leave Here: Mrs. De Casares, 'Queen of Bootleggers,' Forfeits $500 Bond." *New York Times*, May 15, 1927. https:// timesmachine.nytimes.com/timesmachine/1927/05/15/96648769 .html?pageNumber=26.

STELLA BELOUMANT

Minnick, Fred. *Whiskey Women: The Untold Story of How Women Saved Bourbon, Scotch, Irish Whiskey*. Lincoln, NE: Potomac Books, 2013.

JOSEPHINE DOODY

Fraley, John. *Wild River Pioneers: Adventures in the Middle Fork of the Flathead, Great Bear Wilderness, and Glacier National Park*. Whitefish, MT: Big Mountain Publishing, 2008.

Grygo, John. "The Hidden History of Women Bootleggers." UNLV Public History, University of Nevada, Las Vegas, November 4, 2016. https://www .unlvpublichistory.com/the-hidden-history-of-women-bootleggers.

Scott, Tristan. "Doody Homestead Housed 'Bootleg Lady of Glacier Park.'" *Missoulian*, July 22, 2012. https://missoulian.com/lifestyles/territory

/doody-homestead-housed-bootleg-lady-of-glacier-park/article_55a14a20
-d2c0-11e1-ae32-0019bb2963f4.html.

ELIZABETH BÁTHORY
Encyclopaedia Britannica Online, s.v. "Elizabeth Báthory." Accessed
August 17, 2019. https://www.britannica.com/biography/Elizabeth
-Bathory.

"Hungarian Countesses' Torturous Escapades Are Exposed." History.com,
November 13, 2009. Updated December 20, 2019. https://www.history
.com/this-day-in-history/bathorys-torturous-escapades-are-exposed.

GIULIA TOFANA
Carlton, Genevieve. "Meet the Woman Who Poisoned Makeup to Help Over
600 Women Murder Their Husbands." Medium, March 2, 2018. https://
medium.com/@editors_91459/meet-the-woman-who-poisoned-makeup
-to-help-over-600-women-murder-their-husbands-cfb03929c36d.

DARYA SALTYKOVA
Kamenskii, Aleksandr, and David Griffiths. *The Russian Empire in the Eigh-
teenth Century: Tradition and Modernization* (New Russian History).
Oxfordshire, UK: Routledge, 1997.

Klim, Max. *Wife-Killer in the Photo: The Most Cruel Female Maniacs You
Have Not Even Heard Of.* Self-published, 2017.

LAVINIA FISHER
Kennedy, Cynthia M. *Braided Relations, Entwined Lives: The Women of
Charleston's Urban Slave Society.* Bloomington, IN: Indiana Univer-
sity Press, 2005.

Smith, Col. Robert Barr. *Outlaw Women: America's Most Notorious
Daughters, Wives, and Mothers.* Guilford, CT: TwoDot, 2015.

MARIA "GOEIE MIE" SWANENBURG
Glasbergen, Stefan. *Goeie Mie: Biografie van een seriemoordenares.* Leiden, Netherlands: Primavera Pers, 2019.

Hartley, Brandon. "The Deadliest Woman in the Netherlands: Goeie Mie."
DutchNews.nl, October 31, 2019. https://www.dutchnews.nl/fea
tures/2019/10/the-deadliest-woman-in-the-netherlands-goeie-mie/.

"JOLLY JANE" TOPPAN
Bilis, Madeline. "Throwback Thursday: The Arrest of Boston's Murderous
Nursemaid." *Boston Magazine*, October 29, 2015. https://www.boston
magazine.com/news/2015/10/29/jane-toppan/.

"Jane Toppan." Crime Museum. Accessed March 3, 2020. https://www
.crimemuseum.org/crime-library/serial-killers/jane-toppan/.

McBrayer, Mary Kay. *America's First Female Serial Killer: Jane Toppan and the Making of a Monster.* Miami: Mango, 2020.

Schechter, Harold. *Fatal: The Poisonous Life of a Female Serial Killer.* New York: Simon & Schuster, 2003.

ELIZABETH CRESSWELL

Arnold, Catharine. *City of Sin: London and Its Vices.* New York: Simon & Schuster, 2010.

Jordan, Don. *The King's City: A History of London During the Restoration: The City That Transformed a Nation.* New York: Pegasus Books, 2018.

AH TOY

Ditmore, Melissa Hope, ed. *Encyclopedia of Prostitution and Sex Work.* Vol. 1. Westport, CT: Greenwood Publishing Group, 2006.

Liberatore, Karen Peterson. "A Gutsy Chinese 'Working Girl' in Gold Rush San Francisco." *SF Gate,* January 18, 1998. https://www.sfgate.com /books/article/A-Gutsy-Chinese-Working-Girl-in-Gold-Rush-San-3015737 .php.

Pryor, Alton. *Fascinating Women in California History.* Roseville, CA: Stagecoach Publishing, 2014.

KATE ELDER

Enss, Chris. *According to Kate: The Legendary Life of Big Nose Kate, Love of Doc Holliday.* Guilford, CT: TwoDot, 2019.

Guinn, Jeff. *The Last Gunfight: The Real Story of the Shootout at the O.K. Corral—And How It Changed the American West.* New York: Simon & Schuster, 2012.

PEARL DE VERE

Dallas, Sandra. *Colorado Ghost Towns and Mining Camps.* Norman, OK: University of Oklahoma Press, 1985.

Snodgrass, Mary Ellen. *Settlers of the American West: The Lives of 231 Notable Pioneers.* Jefferson, NC: McFarland & Company, 2015.

ADA AND MINNA EVERLEIGH

Abbott, Karen. *Sin in the Second City: Madams, Ministers, Playboys, and the Battle for America's Soul.* New York: Random House, 2008.

"Elevating the World's Oldest Profession in Chicago." *Weekend Edition Saturday,* NPR, July 21, 2007. https://www.npr.org/templates/story/story .php?storyId=12069637.

Kiernan, Louise. "The Everleigh Club." *Chicago Tribune,* December 19,

2007. https://www.chicagotribune.com/nation-world/chi-chicagodays
-everleighclub-story-story.html.

FANNIE PORTER

Patterson, Richard M. *Butch Cassidy: A Biography*. Lincoln, NE: Bison
Books, 1998.

Selcer, Richard F. *Hell's Half Acre: The Life and Legend of a Red-Light
District*. Fort Worth, TX: Texas Christian University Press, 1991.

TILLY DEVINE

"Bad Beef." *Western Mail*. April 4, 1929. https://trove.nla.gov.au/newspa
per/article/38881265.

Irving, Baiba, and Judith Allen. "Devine, Matilda Mary (Tilly) (1900–1970)."
Australian Dictionary of Biography, 1981. http://adb.anu.edu.au/biogra
phy/devine-matilda-mary-tilly-5970.

"Wounded By Razor." *Brisbane Courier*, March 24, 1925. https://trove.nla
.gov.au/newspaper/article/20917429.

PAULINE TABOR

"Kentucky's Most Famous Madam Dead at 87." Associated Press, June 10,
1992. https://apnews.com/04cbcf09183856d3abe7b8be58d08176.

Mink, Jenna. "Grandma Pauline Tabor 'Morphed into a Madam.'" *Bowling
Green Daily News*, September 13, 2012.

Tabor, Pauline. *Pauline's: Memoirs of the Madam on Clay Street*. New
York: Touchstone, 1971.

MARY FIELDS

Blakemore, Erin. "Meet Stagecoach Mary, the Daring Black Pioneer Who
Protected Wild West Stagecoaches." History.com, February 5, 2019.
https://www.history.com/news/meet-stagecoach-mary-the-daring-black
-pioneer-who-protected-wild-west-stagecoaches.

Encyclopaedia Britannica Online, s.v. "Mary Fields." Accessed December 2, 2019. https://www.britannica.com/biography/Mary-Fields.

BELLE STARR

Shirley, Glen. *Belle Starr and Her Times: The Literature, the Facts, and
the Legends*. Norman, OK: University of Oklahoma Press, 1990.

KATE "MA" BARKER

Encyclopaedia Britannica Online, s.v. "Ma Barker." Accessed January 12,
2019. https://www.britannica.com/biography/Ma-Barker.

Enss, Chris, and Howard Kazanjian. *Ma Barker: America's Most Wanted
Mother*. Guilford, CT: TwoDot, 2016.

Smyth, Mitchell. "Town Where Ma Barker Died Sure That Alligator Did Her In." *Chicago Tribune*, October 19, 1986. https://www.chicagotribune.com/news/ct-xpm-1986-10-19-8603190027-story.html.

LAURA "THE THORNY ROSE" BULLION

Lackmann, Ron. *Women of the Western Frontier in Fact, Fiction and Film*. Jefferson, NC: McFarland & Company, 2006.

MacKell, Jan. *Red Light Women of the Rocky Mountains*. Albuquerque, NM: University of New Mexico Press, 2009.

Schwartz, Heather E. *Outlaws, Gunslingers, and Thieves*. Minneapolis, MN: Lerner Publishing Group, 2017.

PEARL HART

"Bandit Pearl Hart Holds Up an Arizona Stagecoach." History.com. Accessed March 2, 2020. https://www.history.com/this-day-in-history/pearl-hart-holds-up-an-arizona-stagecoach.

Rutter, Michael. *Bedside Book of Bad Girls: Outlaw Women of the American West*. Helena, MT: Farcountry Press, 2008.

ROSE DUNN

Smith, Col. Robert Barr. *Outlaw Women: America's Most Notorious Daughters, Wives, and Mothers*. Guilford, CT: TwoDot, 2015.

Wellman, Paul. *A Dynasty of Western Outlaws*. Lincoln, NE: University of Nebraska Press, 1986.

ETTA PLACE

Lee, Honor. *Etta Misplaced: The Story of Etta Place: The Woman Who Was Much More Than the Sundance Kid's Girlfriend*. Bloomington, IN: AuthorHouse, 2013.

Wunder Wall, Linda. *Crossing Trails with the Elusive Outlaw Etta Place*. Independently published, 2019.

LILLIAN SMITH

"Biography: Lillian Smith." PBS. Accessed March 2, 2020. https://www.pbs.org/wgbh/americanexperience/features/oakley-smith/.

Bricklin, Julia. *America's Best Female Sharpshooter: The Rise and Fall of Lillian Frances Smith*. Norman, OK: University of Oklahoma Press, 2017.

Bricklin, Julia. "The Faux 'Sioux' Sharpshooter Who Became Annie Oakley's Rival." *Smithsonian*, May 8, 2017. https://www.smithsonianmag.com/history/faux-sioux-sharpshooter-who-became-annie-oakleys-rival-180963164/.

Hudson, Angela Pulley. *Real Native Genius: How an Ex-Slave and a White Mormon Became Famous Indians*. Chapel Hill, NC: The University of North Carolina Press, 2015.

BONNIE PARKER

"Bonnie and Clyde." FBI.gov. Accessed March 2, 2020. https://www.fbi.gov /history/famous-cases/bonnie-and-clyde.

Guinn, Jeff. "The Irresistible Bonnie Parker." *Smithsonian*, April 2009. https://www.smithsonianmag.com/history/the-irresistible-bonnie -parker-59411903/.

Schneider, Paul. *Bonnie and Clyde: The Lives Behind the Legend*. New York: St. Martin's Griffin, 2010.

MARIE BAKER

Puck, Kristy. "10 Notorious Female Gangsters." *Mental Floss*, September 1, 2014. https://www.mentalfloss.com/article/58626/10-female-gangsters -you-should-know-about.

REABLE CHILDS AND THE GOREE GIRLS

Hollandsworth, Skip. "O Sister, Where Art Thou?" *Texas Monthly*, May 2003. https://www.texasmonthly.com/articles/o-sister-where-art-thou/.

PRINCESS CARABOO

Johnson, Catherine. *The Curious Tale of the Lady Caraboo*. New York: Corgi Children's, 2015.

Jones, Paul Anthony. "The Mysterious 19th Century 'Princess' Who Fooled a Town." *Mental Floss*, March 8, 2017. https://www.mentalfloss.com /article/92250/mysterious-19th-century-princess-who-fooled-town -thinking-she-was-royalty.

LEAH, KATE, AND MAGGIE FOX

Abbott, Karen. "The Fox Sisters and the Rap on Spiritualism." *Smithsonian*, October 30, 2012. https://www.smithsonianmag.com/history/the-fox -sisters-and-the-rap-on-spiritualism-99663697/.

Encyclopaedia Britannica Online, s.v. "Margaret Fox and Catherine Fox." Accessed March 1, 2020. https://www.britannica.com/biography /Margaret-Fox-and-Catherine-Fox.

Jackson, Herbert G. "Spiritualist Landmark Becomes One Man's 'Calling.'" *New York Times*, March 29, 1970. https://timesmachine.nytimes.com /timesmachine/1970/03/29/90608330.html?pageNumber=323.

CATHAY WILLIAMS

"Cathay Williams." US National Park Service. Updated January 15, 2020. https://www.nps.gov/people/cwilliams.htm.

Rand-Caplan, Ramona. "Cathay Williams (1850–)." BlackPast.org, January 30, 2007. https://www.blackpast.org/african-american-history/williams -cathay-1850/.

"A Soldier's Story: Cathay Williams Defied Her Time to Become the Only

Known Female Buffalo Soldier." Wounded Warrior Project, n.d. Accessed March 4, 2020. https://newsroom.woundedwarriorproject.org/The -Only-Known-Female-Buffalo-Soldier-Cathay-Williams.

ELIZABETH BIGLEY

Abbott, Karen. "The High Priestess of Fraudulent Finance." *Smithsonian*, June 27, 2012. https://www.smithsonianmag.com/history/the-high -priestess-of-fraudulent-finance-45/.

Schwarz, Ted. *Cleveland Curiosities: Eliot Ness & His Blundering Raid, a Busker's Promise, the Richest Heiress Who Never Lived and More.* Mount Pleasant, SC: Arcadia Publishing, 2010.

"Top 10 Imposters: Cassie Chadwick." *Time*, May 26, 2009. http://content .time.com/time/specials/packages/article/0,28804,1900621_1900618 _1900852,00.html.

NOTES

Introduction

1. FBI Crime Clock. https://ucr.fbi.gov/crime-in-the-u.s/2017
/crime-in-the-u.s.-2017/topic-pages/crime-clock.

Ingela Gathenhielm
The Swedish Privateer Who Had the King's Blessing

1. *Encyclopaedia Britannica Online*, s.v. "Privateer," accessed October 30, 2018.

Anne Bonny
The Pirate Who Pleaded Pregnant

1. Marcus Rediker, *Villains of All Nations: Atlantic Pirates in the Golden Age* (Boston: Beacon Press, 2005).
2. Tony Bartelme, "The True and False Stories of Anne Bonny, Pirate Woman of the Caribbean," *Post and Courier*, November 21, 2018.
3. *Encyclopaedia Britannica Online*, s.v. "Mary Read," accessed June 26, 2019.

Ching Shih
The Formidable Pirate Princess

1. Paul A. Van Dyke, "Floating Brothels and the Canton Flower Boats 1750–1930," *Review of Culture*, International Edition no. 37 (January 2011): 112–42, https://www.researchgate.net/publication/328380053_Floating_Brothels_and_the_Canton_Flower_Boats_1750-1930.

Eleanor "Madame Moustache" Dumont
The Gambler Who Fell Victim to a Broken Heart

1. Alton Pryor, *Fascinating Women in California History* (Roseville, CA: Stagecoach Publishing, 2014).

Lottie Deno
The Faro Queen Who Charmed the South

1. Chris Enss, *Wicked Women: Notorious, Mischievous, and Wayward Ladies from the Old West* (Guilford, CT: TwoDot, 2015).

NOTES

Willie Carter Sharpe
The Speedster with Diamonds in Her Teeth
1. Greg Toppo, "'Moonshine' Tracks Centuries-Old U.S. Whiskey Trail," *USA Today*, July 18, 2014.

Maggie Bailey
The Queen of Mountain Bootleggers
1. Melissa Block, "'Queen of the Mountain Bootleggers' Maggie Bailey," December 8, 2005, on *All Things Considered*, NPR.
2. Block, "'Queen of the Mountain Bootleggers' Maggie Bailey."
3. Block, "'Queen of the Mountain Bootleggers' Maggie Bailey."

Gloria de Casares
The Scotch Queen of the Seas
1. Fred Minnick, "Women's History Month Spotlight: Women Bootleggers," *Huffington Post*, March 10, 2014.
2. "Overstays Her Leave Here: Mrs. De Casares, 'Queen of Bootleggers,' Forfeits $500 Bond," *New York Times*, May 15, 1927.

Stella Beloumant
The Bootlegger Taken Down After a 24-Hour Stakeout
1. Fred Minnick, *Whiskey Women: The Untold Story of How Women Saved Bourbon, Scotch, and Irish Whiskey* (Lincoln, NE: Potomac Books, 2013).

Josephine Doody
The Bootleg Lady of Glacier Park
1. Tristan Scott, "Doody Homestead Housed 'Bootleg Lady of Glacier Park,'" *Missoulian*, July 22, 2012.

Giulia Tofana
The Cosmetics Killer
1. Paul Aron, ed., *Mysteries in History: From Prehistory to the Present* (Goleta, CA: ABC-CLIO, 2005).

"Jolly Jane" Toppan
The Sadistic Nurse
1. Harold Schechter, *Fatal: The Poisonous Life of a Female Serial Killer* (New York: Simon & Schuster, 2003).
2. Schechter, *Fatal*.
3. Jennifer Myers, "For 10 Years, 'Jolly Jane' Poured Her Poison," *Lowell Sun*, November 2, 2011.

NOTES

Elizabeth Cresswell
The Madam Who Lived "Well"

1. Don Jordan, *The King's City: A History of London During the Restoration: The City That Transformed a Nation* (New York: Pegasus Books, 2018).
2. Catharine Arnold, *City of Sin: London and Its Vices* (New York: Simon & Schuster, 2010).

Ah Toy
The Entrepreneurial Madam

1. Chris Enss, "Wild Women of the West: Ah-Toy," *Cowgirl*, April 9, 2019.
2. Karen Peterson Liberatore, "A Gutsy Chinese 'Working Girl' in Gold Rush San Francisco," *SF Gate*, January 18, 1998.
3. Enss, "Wild Women of the West: Ah-Toy."

Pauline Tabor
The Madam with Two Lifestyles

1. Jenna Mink, "Grandma Pauline Tabor 'Morphed into a Madam,'" *Bowling Green Daily News*, September 13, 2012.

Pearl Hart
The "Lady Bandit" of the Wild West

1. Michael Rutter, *Bedside Book of Bad Girls: Outlaw Women of the American West* (Helena, MT: Farcountry Press, 2008).

Rose Dunn
The Woman Who Allegedly Ran Through Bullets for Love

1. Robert G. McCubbin, "Who Is Rose of Cimarron?" *True West Magazine*, May 2005.

Bonnie Parker
You Know, *That* Bonnie

1. Jeff Guinn, "The Irresistible Bonnie Parker," *Smithsonian*, April 2009.

Reable Childs and the Goree Girls
The Women Who Sang Their Way Out of Prison

1. Skip Hollandsworth, "O Sister, Where Art Thou?" *Texas Monthly*, May 2003.